The 1833 LAND LOTTERY

of

GEORGIA

and

Other Missing Names *of* Winners

in the Georgia Land Lotteries

By:

Robert S. Davis, Jr.

Copyright 1991
By: Southern Historical Press, Inc.

All rights reserved. No part of this publication may be reproduced, stored in a retrieval system, transmitted in any form, posted on to the web in any form or by any means without the prior written permission of the publisher.

Please direct all correspondence and orders to:

www.southernhistoricalpress.com
or
SOUTHERN HISTORICAL PRESS, Inc.
PO BOX 1267
375 West Broad Street
Greenville, SC   29601
southernhistoricalpress@gmail.com

ISBN #0-89308-338-0

Dedicated to

the Memory of

Jewell Dyer

INTRODUCTION

Farris Cadle, author of an upcoming book on the history of Georgia land grants and surveys, discovered a Georgia law of 1833 that ordered the fractional (less than 40 acres) land lots of the 1832 Georgia Gold Land Lot Lottery to be drawn from the remaining (losing) tickets of the two 1832 land lotteries.

A search of the Georgia Surveyor General Department has turned up the list of some 1,500 Georgia citizens who won the lots dispensed in the forgotten 1833 land lottery. Reproduced below are the names and other information on those land lots and their winners. The original of this list is the last document on microfilm reel 286/49 at the Georgia Department of Archives and History. Also given away in this land lottery were a handful of lots left over from previous land lotteries. For information on abbreviations used in designating participants in the 1832 land lotteries see James F. Smith, The 1832 (Cherokee Lnd Lottery) (1838; rep. ed., 1976). For a summary of the history of Georgia's land lotteries and the qualifications for each. see Robert S. Davis, Jr., Georgia Genealogical Workbook (1987), pp. 56-9.

Also included in the list below are more than thirty land lots ommitted from the original drawing of the 1820 Georgia land lottery. These lots are designated with "1820LL". This list appears at the end of the list of Houston County land lots on microfilm reel 286/47 at the Georgia Department of Archives and History. These lots were drawn for and given to participants in the 1820 land lottery.

NAME/DIST., & COUNTY OF RESIDENCE/BUYER IF LOT REVERTED/DATE GRANTED/LOT/DISTRICT/SECT.

CROUCH GEORGE--Paces, Putnam County--S. W. Horne--5 Jan 1847--1F--(22.5 Acres)--1-1Cher.

WATSON TYRE--Higginbothams, Carrol Co.--17 Apr 34 (Granted Twice)--2F (9.9 Acres)--1--1Cher.

WATSON TYRE--(Same lot granted twice)--Wynn A.B.--26 March 1841--2F--1--1Cher.

IVY EPHRAIM SENT.--Lynns, Warren County--4 May 1841--3F (38.5 Acres)--1--1Cher.

MERIDITH SAMUEL JR.--Blounts, Wilkinson Co.--A.B. Wynn--26 Mar 46--4F (2.25 Ac)--1--1Cher.

JACKSON EDMUND--147, Greene County--T. Cherry--9 Feb 1846--5F (13.3 Acres)--1--1Cher.

JOHNSON ELIJAH--Phillips, Talbot County--10 December 1834--6F (29.2 Acres)--1--1Cher.

SPENCE MCCALVIS H.--Towers, Gwinnett Co.--9 December 1834--7F (13.2 Acres)--1--1Cher.

FERGUSON ISAAC--Colliers, Monroe County--Not Granted--8F (1.3 Acres)--1--1Cher.

KEY HENRY--Norris, Monroe County--31 December 1833--9F (32.4 Acres)--1--1Cher.

RILEY ELIZABETH (Widow)--122, Richmond Co.--1 November 1834--10F (24.2 Acres)--1--1Cher.

ARNOLD WILLIAM--Jacks, Clarke County--28 November 1840--11F (4.2 Acres)--1--1Cher.

BRAWNER HENRY SR.--Howell, Elbert County--29 March 1834--12F (39.4 Acres)--1--1Cher.

THOMPSON RICHARD--Blackstocks, Hall County--25 Feb 1834--13F (37.3 Acres)--1--1Cher.

SINQUEFIELD MARY (Widow)--Sinquefields, Washington Co.--6 Aug 1834--14F (37 Acres)--1--1Cher.

PARKER WILLIAM--608th, Taliaferro County--18 December 1834--15F (36.5 Acres)--1--1Cher.

DIFERNATTE REUBEN R.--374th, Putnam County--21 Feb 1834--16F (39.75 Acres)--1--1Cher.

BEANCHAMP JOHN--Halls, Butts County--J.A. Sands--31 May 1846--17F (2.5 Acres)--1--1Cher.

BARROW WILLIAM JR.--Bealls, Burke County--15 October 1835--18F (26 Acres)--1--1Cher.

LARRANCE JOAB--Jones, Madison County--17 November 1836--19F (39.9 Acres)--1--1Cher.

MCNEEL WILLIAM--McClains, Newton County--21 March 1834--20F (13 Acres)--1--1Cher.

SCOTT WILLIAM--Justices, Bibb County--18 November 1834--21F (37 Acres)--1--1Cher.

CROCKETT JAMES W.--Colquhouns, Henry County--21 March 1834--22F (33.5 Acres)--1--1Cher.

HOWELL WILLIAM--Edwards, Talbot County--Not Granted)--23F (.8 Acres)--1--1Cher.

HOBBS WILLIAM H.--Colliers, Monroe County--26 April 1834--24F (10.75 Acres)--1--1Cher.

BASS ROWEL R.--Britts, Randolph County--21 March 1834--25F (28 Acres)--1--1Cher.

KENNAMORE DAVID--Jones, Habersham County--21 March 1834--26F (21.2 Acres)--1--1Cher.

HORN WHITINGTON--Brocks, Muscogee County--17 December 1835--27F (6.4 Acres)--1--1Cher.

NICHOLSON ISAAC--Higginbothams, Rabun County--13 May 1835--28F (39 Acres)--1-1Cher.

FORRESTER GEORGE B.--271th, McIntosh County--24 June 1834--29F (22.4 Acres)--1--1Cher.

PIERCE SAMPSON--Says, Hall County--Not Granted--30F (1.2 Acres)--1--1Cher.

ADAMS JOHN--Deans, DeKalb County--18 February 1834--31F (20.2 Acres)--1--1Cher.

SMITH WILLIAM F.--374th, Putnam County--7 November--32F (32.1 Acres)--1--1Cher.

WHITEHEAD RICHARD--Streetmans, Twiggs County--7 Nov 1834--33F (34.6 Acres)--1--1Cher.

MILLICAN HUGH--Wilsons, Pike County--25 April 1834--34F (39 Acres)--1--1Cher.

LAY SAMPSON--Ridens, Jackson Co.--7 Nov 1834--35F (2.5 Acres Waters Ferry)--1--1Cher.

THWEATT W.W.--Fews, Muscogee Co.--29 Apr 1837--36F (14.6 Acres Waters Ferry)--1--1Cher.

PEARCE JOHN SR.--Griffins, Fayette County--7 Nov. 1834--37F (25.2 Acres)--1--1Cher.

BRYAN, SAMUEL J.--1st, Chatham County--29 April 1834--38F (39.1 Acres)--1--1Cher.

CRAWFORD ARTHUR--Mucks, Hall County--16 June 1835--39F (4.3 Acres)--1--1Cher.

CARTER THOMAS J.--Griffins, Hall County--7 November 1834--40F (24.8 Acres)--1--1Cher.

HOLCOMB THOMAS--Martins, Hall County--17 November 1834--41F (38.7 Acres)--1--1Cher.

BONNER JAMES--319th, Baldwin County--7 March 1834--42F (15.2 Acres)--1--1Cher.

JONES ELIZABETH (Widow)--Currys, Wilkinson Co.--27 Feb 1835--43F (26 Acres)--1--1Cher.

GALLOWAY JAMES--Whipples, Wilkinson County--13 March 1834--44F (39 Acres)--1--1Cher.

STRANGE WILLIAM--Catletts, Franklin County--11 December 1834--45F (20 Acres)--1--1Cher.

YARBOROUGH LEWIS--Moffetts, Muscogee County--27 Feb 1835--46F (15 Acres)--1--1Cher.

MURRAY JAMES H.W.--Penrifoys, Henry Co.--1 September 1834--47F (25 Acres)--1--1Cher.

PATTERSON WILLIAM--Morrisons, Appling Co.--10 November 1834--48F (32 Acres)--1-1Cher.

MILLER JAMES--Heedons, Hall Co.--31 May 1834--49F (32.4 Acres Rogers Ferry)--1--1Cher.

HARP EDWARD--Gittens, Fayette Co.--30 Jan 1837--50F (23.3 Acres)--1--1Cher.

PITMAN RENE M.--406th, Gwinnett County--6 April 1835--51F (13.3 Acres)--1--1Cher.

CARSON, JAMES J.--Phillips, Talbot County--30 January 1835--52F (2.2 Acres)--1--1Cher.

BROWN JOHN D.--Garners, Washington Co.--7 May 1835--53F (37.8 Acres)--1--1Cher.

MILES JARED--McDowells, Lincoln Co.--20 Aug 1835--54F (31.2 Acres)--1--1Cher.

WAITS JACOB--406, Gwinnett Co.--10 Nov 1834--55F (19.3 Acres)--1--1Cher.

HASTING BENJAMIN--Brooks, Muscogee Co.--15 Dec 1835--56F (2.2 Acres)--1--1Cher.

TANNER JOSEPH--Williams, Washington Co.--7 Jan 1836--57F (23.3 Acres)--1--1Cher.

GLOVER JOHN--Hintons, Wilkes Co.--26 Dec 1835--58F (38.5 Acres)--1--1Cher.

PETERMAN HENRY G.--Jenkins, Oglethorpe Co.--30 Dec 1833--59F (13.4 Acres)--1--1Cher.
LESTER JOHN--Butts, Monroe Co.--17 Jan 1834--60F (39.2 Acres)--1--1Cher.
NASH EDWARD L.--Johnsons, DeKalb Co.--19 Mar 1835--61F (24 Acres)--1--1Cher.
TATE WILLIAM--Ross, Monroe Co.--29 Sep 1834--62F (3 Acres Collins Ferry)--1--1Cher.
ALLEN CYRUS--Woodruffs, Campbell Co.--16 Apr 1834--63F (35.5 Acres)--1--1Cher.
McDUGALL MILES E.--McClures, Rabun Co.--29 Mar 1834--64F (6.7 Acres)--1--1Cher.
FORT CHARLES M.--Christies, Jefferson Co.--5 July 1834--65F (5.6 Acres)--1--1Cher.
PETTIBONE SARAH wid.--3rd, Chatham Co.--6 Dec 1834--66F (26 Acres)--1--1Cher.
WATKINS JOHN--192, Elbert Co.--9 Dec 1834--67F (38 Acres)--1--1Cher.
GILLISPIE JOHN P.--Higginbothams, Carroll Co.--21 Feb 1834--68F (7.7 Acres)--1--1Cher.
WELCH MICHAEL--Whitakers, Crawford Co.--21 Feb 1834--69F (39.1 Acres)--1--1Cher.
SCAIFE WILLIAM JR.--Mobleys, DeKalb Co.--9 Dec 1834--70F (25.2 Acres)--1--1Cher.
RUTHERFORD RICHARD orps.--Roystons, Franklin Co.--24 Oct 1834--71F (38.6 Acres)--1--1Cher.
NEELY WILLIAM--Mucks, Hall Co.--4 July 1835--72F (29 Acres)--1--1 Cher.
CABOS JOHN--Clelands, Chatham Co.--21 June 1834--73F (39.5 Acres)--1--1Cher.
MELL BENJAMIN (Orphans)--15, Liberty Co.--9 Feb 1835--74F (38.6 Acres)--1--1Cher.
LAMBERT JOHN--Baileys, Laurens Co.--27 Jan 1835--75F (39.2 Acres)--1--1Cher.
PENN WILLIAM S.--Beasleys, Ogle Co.--29 Jan 1836--76F (3.2 Ac. Gilbert's Fy.)--1--1Cher.
HAWTHORN JONATHAN C.--720, Decatur Co.--25 May 1837--864 (30.9 Acres)--2--1Cher.
WILLIAMS ARINGTON B.--Griffins, Fayette Co.--11 Aug 1834--864 (20 Acres)--2--1Cher.
BROWN JOHN D.--Garners, Washington Co.--1 Jan 1834--936 (18.6 Acres)--2--1Cher.
BRAWNER WILLIAM--Crawfords, Morgan Co.--25 Nov 1834--937 (13.5 Acres)--2--1Cher.
KOLB PHILIP--Sanderlins, Chatham Co.--9 Dec 1834--1007 (30.75 Acres)--2--1Cher.
STEPHENS ANDREW B. orps.--588, Upson Co.--20 Jun 1843--1008 (108) (1.5 Acres)--2--1Cher.

JOHNSON HENRY--Allens, Bibb Co.--1Apr 1835--1009 (1.5 Acres)--2--1Cher.

SMITH ROBERT--Smiths, Houston Co.--9 Dec 1834--1010 (27 Acres)--2--1Cher.

BAKER ABNER--Crows, Pike Co.--11 Jan 1834--1077 (10 Acres)--2--1Cher.

BRACK WILLIAM--Bailey, Laurens Co.--30 July 1834--1078 (6 Acres)--2--1Cher.

WILSON ELIZABETH (Widow)--605th, Taliaferro Co.--6 Feb 1835--1144 (29.5 Acres)--2--1Cher.

BLACKWILL JAMES B.--Seays, Hall Co.--12 May 1836--1145 (22 Acres)--2--1Cher.

DICKSON JOHN--55, Emanuel Co.--11 May 1837--1210 (22 Acres)--2--1 Cher.

COWARD WILLIAM--Brewtons, Tattnall Co.--2 May 1835--1211 (9 Acres)--2--1Cher.

MITCHELL PETER--Taylors, Jones Co.--24 Mar 1837--1276 (8 Acres)--2--1Cher.

McLEOD HUGH orphan--Bazemore, Jones Co.--No date given--1F (14 Acres)--4--1Cher.

STEWART J.--McLins, Butts Co.--C. Day--9 May 1846--2F (14 Acres)--4--1Cher.

KIRKPATRICK HARMAN--Hargroves, Newton Co. (B.T. Bethune)--30 Mar 1846--3F (14 Ac.)--4--1Cher.

STINCHCOMB PHILIIP--Fenns, Clarke Co.--23 Nov 1843--4F (14 Acres)--4--1Cher.

SANSING JOHN SR.--Smiths, Henry Co.--29 Jan 1835--5F (14 Acres)--4--1Cher.

STEEL DENNIS JR.--Towers, Gwinnett Co.--L.W. Cooper--21 Nov 1853--6F (14 Acres)--4--1Cher.

McKINNEY ROBERT D.--34, Scriven Co.--J. Parr--7 July 1846--7F (14 Acres)--4--1Cher.

RICHERSON THOMAS--Griffins, DeKalb Co.--30 June 1843--8F (14 Acres)--4--1Cher.

EUBANKS JOHN SR.--Hollidays, Jackson Co.--11 May 1839--9F (14 Acres)--4--1Cher.

SPENCER JAMES J.W.--9th, Effingham Co.--No date given--10F (14 Acres)--4--1Cher.

GARNER JOHN N.--Albersons, Walton Co.--No date given--11F (14 Acres)--4--1Cher.

BURNSIDE ELEANOR wid.--561, Upson Co.--4 Apr 1911 Sold by Ory. Dawson Co.--12F--4--1Cher.

HICKLIN ELIZABETH wid.--Everetts, Washington Co.--No date given--13F (14 Ac.)--4--1Cher.

MANGHAM JAMES W.--Thaxtons, Butts Co.--Orphny Wilson--17 Dec. 1845--14F (14 Ac.)--4--1Cher.

WHITE JAMES--Hughes, Habersham Co.--19 Jan 1836--15F (14 Acres)--4--1Cher.

TIMMONS SAMUEL--Wheelers, Pulaski Co.--5 Aug 1837--16F (14 Acres)--4--1Cher.

BEALL ALEXANDER R.--Walkers, Columbia Co.--28 Nov 1835--17F (14 Acres)--4--1Cher.

STARRET BENJAMIN--Sewells, Franklin Co.--5 Mar 1838--18F (14 Acres)--4--1Cher.

KING BERRY--Hammonds, Franklin Co.--13 Nov 1837--19F (14 Acres)--4--1Cher.

VEAL ALLEN G.--Griffins, DeKalb Co.--8 Apr 1843--20F (14 Acres)--4--1Cher.

DENSON RICHARD--Prescotts, Twiggs Co.--1 July 1843--21F (14 Acres)--4--1Cher.

STOWERS HENRY--Hendons, Carroll Co.--1 July 1843--22F (14 Acres)--4--1Cher.

CARR JOHN--Comers, Jones Co.--19 Oct 1837--23F (14 Acres)--4--1Cher.

SPENCE LEWIS--Adams, Columbia Co.--H. Phillips--1 May 1846--24F (14 Acres)--4--1Cher.

REESE REUBEN--Whitakers, Crawford Co.--16 Dec 1834--25F (14 Acres)--4--1Cher.

SOUTHERLAND JOHN--138, Greene Co.--1 July 1833-26F (14 Acres)--4--1Cher.

BURKS WILEY P.--Griers, Meriwether Co.--M.S. Thompson--2-4-47 & 6-15-35--27F--4--1Cher.

BELL, THOMAS--Smiths, Elbert Co.--21 Dec 1838--28F (14 Acres)--4--1Cher.

WILLINGHAM ISAAC JR.--Graves, Lincoln Co.--20 Dec 1838--29F (14 Acres)--4--1Cher.

THORNTON HASTIN G.--687, Lee Co.--W.H. Graham--30 Apr 1846--30F (14 Acres)--4--1Cher.

BLACK, SAMUEL SR.--555, Upson Co.--W.H.Graham--30 Apr 1846--31F (14 Acres)--4--1Cher.

DEWBERRY WILLIAM--Colliers, Monroe Co.--21 Dec 1847--32F (14 Acres)--4--1Cher.

ROSSIE JOHN B.--307, Putnam Co.--10 May 1843--33F (14 Acres)--4--1Cher.

LOWE GEORGE T.--Groces, Bibb Co.--F.P.Hyde--20 May 1846--34F (14 Acres)--4--1Cher.

KIRKLAND SNOWDON--Moseleys, Wilkes Co. (Isaac Hide?)--Not given--35F--(4 Acres)--4--1Cher.

PATE HOLLIS M.--Comptons, Fayette Co.--No date given--36F (12 Acres)--4--1Cher.

HUDSON WILLIAM orphans--Lunsford, Elbert Co.--No date given--37F (12 Acres)--4--1Cher.

BETTERTON WILLIAM--Evans, Fayette Co.--J.W. Looper--8 Sep 1845--38F (12 Acres)--4--1Cher.

BRUMBELO JAMES--Smiths, Campbell Co.--6 Jun 1837--39F (12 Acres)--4--1Cher.

HINES JAMES--Stricklands, Meriwether Co.--9 June 1841--40F (12 Acres)--4--1Cher.

BAXTER JOHN--Whisenhunts, Carroll Co.--25 Aug 1838--41F (12 Acres)--4--1Cher.

CARTER PENDLETON--McGinnis, Jackson Co.--22 Apr 1837--42F (12 Acres)--4--1Cher.

HARVEY ALBERT G.--Rooks, Putnam Co.--1 Oct 1836--43F (12 Acres)--4--1Cher.

FARIS WILLIAM--Kenners, Rabun Co.--14 Nov 1837--44F (12 Acres)--4--1Cher.

FARR MARY wid.--Sanderlins, Chatham Co.--2 Sep 1837--45F (12 Acres)--4--1Cher.

PORNNEL JOHN--Sinquefields, Washington Co.--21 Jan 1840--46F (12 Acres)--4--1Cher.

PIPER JAMES J.--Arringtons, Meriwether Co.--3 Dec 1837--47F (12 Acres)--4--1Cher.

TROUT GILES--2nd Section, Cherokee Co.--L.F. Harris--8 May 1846--48F--4--1Cher.

BARDIN ARTHUR--Not given--12 Nov 1841--(Two grants same lot) (12 Acres)--4--1Cher.

LEONARD WILLIAM--Curries, Meriwether Co.--17 July 1844--49F (See Bardin Arthur)--4--1Cher.

JONES EPHRAIM--Hughs, Habersham Co.--See Resolution of Feb 1953--50F (12 Acres)--4--1Cher.

DURHAM SEABON J.--Brewers, Monroe Co.--12 June 1843--51F (12 Acres)--4--1Cher.

WILLIAMSON JAMES--Wilcoxs, Telfair Co.--29 June 1843--52F (12 Acres)--4--1Cher.

DUKE JOHN T.--Coxes, Morgan Co.--James Cantrell--14 Dec 1849--53F (12 Acres)--4--1Cher.

McGEE WILEY orp. of--Harris, Greene Co.--W.C. Graham--30 Apr 1846--54F (12 Ac.)--4--1Cher.

PARTAIN ROBERT--454, Walton Co.--Not given--55F (12 Acres)--4--1Cher.

WHEAT LEVI--Maguires, Morgan Co.--J.M. Cobb--27 Apr 1846--56F (12 Acres)--4--1Cher.

McGEHEE ABNER--Paces, Putnam Co.--J.H. Smith--20 May 1846--57F (12 Acres)--4--1Cher.

CHAPPELL JEFFERSON--Stricklands, Meri. Co.--John Smith--30 Apr 1846--58F (12 Ac.)--4--1Cher.

HOUSE ZACHARIAH B.--785, Sumter Co.--26 Apr 1836--59F (12 Acres)--4--1Cher.

ROSS JESSE M.--Taylors, Jones Co. (W.A. Carr)--20 May 1846--60F (12 Acres)--4--1Cher.

WALDRUM DAVID M.--Smiths, Houston Co. (William Martin)--6-10-1848--61F (12 Ac.)--4--1Cher.

McLEOD ARCHIBALD--Graves, Thomas Co.--N.M. Feely--7 July 1846--62F (12 Ac.)--4--1Cher.

Butler John--Derings, Henry Co.--Not given--63F (12 Acres)--4--1Cher.

GRAVES SOLOMON--Stantons, Newton Co.--6 Nov 1838--64F (12 Acres)--4--1Cher.

RUFF WILLIAM--Derings, Henry Co.--Not given--65F (12 Acres)--4--1Cher.

HARRIS HANNAH wid.--Stantons, Newton Co.--22 Sep 1842--66F (12 Acres)--4--1Cher.

LANCE JOHN R. minor--Jones, Habersham Co.--B.F. Goss--2-12-1855--67F (12 Acres)--4--1Cher.

WHITE ROBERT--Swineys, Laurens Co.--Reuben T. Burt--12 May 1848--68F (12 Acres)--4--1Cher.

JACKSON JAMES A.--141, Greene Co.--James Hyde--15 May 1848--69F (12 Acres)--4--1Cher.

HODGES NANCY wid.--Bracketts, Newton Co.--James Hyde--15 May 1848--70F (12 Ac.)--4--1Cher.

WALLACE DAVID C.--Brewers, Monroe Co.--Not given--71F (12 Acres)--4--1Cher.

BURNETT THOMAS--Silmans, Pike Co.--9 June 1834--864 (39 Acres)--12--1Cher.

HASELETT JOHN--Youngs, Carroll Co.--20 Mar 1834--869 (38.5 Acres)--12--1Cher.

BUCHANNAN BENJAMIN B.--Evans, Laurens Co.--6 Mar 1834--878 (35 Acres)--12--1Cher.

WELCH EDWARD--Pates, Warren Co.--8 July 1834--879 (20 Acres)--12--1Cher.

JORDAN ELIAS--Pearces, Houston Co.--1 Mar 1834--880 (32 Acres)--12--1Cher.

SMITH EDY wid.--Gunns, Jones Co.--1 Mar 1834--881 (30 Acres)--12--1Cher.

BARNETT CALVIN--Burgess, Carroll Co.--4 Feb 1834--882 (6.2 Acres)--12--1Cher.

BRAZILE ELIZABETH wid.--Currys, Wilkinson Co.--26 Dec 1833--883 (33.7 Acres)--12--1Cher.

COAL ISAAC--Durhams, Talbot Co.--29 Mar 1833--936 (38.5 Acres)--12--1Cher.

DEATON WILLIAM JR.--Deatons, Jackson Co.--24 Dec 1836--938 (38.4 Acres)--12--1Cher.

PRICHARD PLEASANT--Stokes, Lincoln Co.--27 Dec 1836--939 (1.5 Acres)--12--1Cher.

REYNOLDS GABRIEL--106, Hancock Co.--13 May 1834--940 (15.6 Acres)--12--1Cher.

DUPREE BURGES--Tompkins, Putnam Co.--7 Jan 1835--941 (39.1 Acres)--12--1Cher.

JOHNSON BRYANT--Bryants, Pulaski Co.--17 Nov 1841--942 (1/16 Acre)--12--1Cher.

BRADLEY WILLIAM D.--Hintons, Wilkes Co.--16 Dec 1835--943 (31.5 Acres)--12--1Cher.

SAXON JOHN M.--192, Elbert Co.--21 Aug 1834--991 (38.9 Acres)--12--1Cher.

DIAL MARTIN SR.--Albersons, Walton Co.--24 Dec 1833--992 (38.5 Acres)--12--1Cher.

COLIAR WILLIAM--761, Heard Co.--8 Aug 1834--1040 (19.7 Acres)--12--1Cher.

BRYANT WILEY--Tuggles, Meriwether Co.--28 Aug 1834--1041 (7.5 Acres)--12--1Cher.

MAXWELL JOEL--R. Browns, Habersham Co.--3 Apr 1834--1042 (29 Acres)--12--1Cher.

WALLACE WILLIAM SR.--Petersons, Burke Co.--22 Mar 1841--1043 (38.5 Acres)--12--1Cher.

ASHWORTH JOB--Mangums, Franklin Co.--6 May 1834--1093 (30 Acres)--12--1Cher.

DAVIS ADAM--Willis, Franklin Co.--15 Mar 1834--1094 (32.5 Acres)--12--1Cher.

MYLAM LEWIS--Hills, Harris Co.--22 Apr 1834--1140 (35 Acres)--12--1Cher.

SIZEMORE HENRY--Burgess, Carroll Co.--1 July 1823--1141 (32 Acres)--12--1Cher.

ECHOLS ELIJAH V.--Higginbothams, Rabun Co.--4 May 1837--1882 (10 Acres)--12--1Cher.

MACINTOSH RODRICK--Petersons, Montgomery Co.--25 Mar 1834--1183 (8.5 Acres)--12--1Cher.

ALLEN WILLIAM M.B.--Robinsons, Putnam Co.--31 July 1834--1884 (One Acre)--12--1Cher.

TWILLEY JAMES--Aderholds, Campbell Co.--1 Apr 1834--1185 (5 Acres)--12--1Cher.

TREADWELL ISAAC--Brewers, Walton Co.--23 Jan 1834--1186 (11.5 Acres)--12--1Cher.

HANN WILLIAM--Philips, Monroe Co.--16 Feb 1843--1187 (2.5 Acres)--12--1Cher.

STOVALL OZIAS--Belchers, Jasper Co.--22 May 1838--1188 (0.5 Acre)--12--1Cher.

PUCKETT JOHN--Whitakers, Crawford Co.--25 June 1834--1189 (1.9 Acres)--12--1Cher.

COPPIDGE CHARLES--Allisons, Pike Co.--1 July 1843--1190 (8.7 Acres)--12--1Cher.

SLATTER WILLIAM C.--Fews, Muscogee Co.--13 June 1843--1191 (5.5 Acres)--12--1Cher.

MELTON KINCHEN--Olivers, Twiggs Co.--27 Nov 1834--1192 (2.5 Acres)--12--1Cher.

WILLIAMS JAMES R.--Fulks, Wilkes Co.--J.F. Cooper--25 Nov 1845--1193 (0.2 Acres)--12--1Cher.

DELONY ROBERT J.--Millers, Camden Co.--16 Nov 1837--1194 (18 Acres)--12--1Cher.

CONNER WILSON--36, Scriven Co.--21 Jan 1834--1198 (28.4 Acres)--12--1Cher.

THIGPEN JAMES--Robisons, Washington Co.--17 July 1834--1199 (2 Acres)--12--1Cher.
CRUTCHFIELD STAPLETON--Gunns, Jones Co.--28 Nov 1839--1200 (4.5 Acres)--12--1Cher.
HUTCHINSON JAMES G.--Huchinsons, Columbia Co.--28 June 1843--1201 (38.8 Acres)--12--1Cher.
LEWIS WILLIAM F.--Mullins, Carroll Co.--11 Jan 1834--1202 (22.1 Acres)--12--1Cher.
TURNER GREEN B. H.--Dearings, Butts Co.--29 Sep 1834--1203 (4.25 Acres)--12--1Cher.
SEARS DAVID C.--Smiths, Wilkinson Co.--8 Mar 1834--1204 (11.1 Acres)--12--1Cher.
RED JAMES orphs.--Davis, Gwinnett Co.--11 Nov 1835--1205 (21.5 Acres)--12--1Cher.
DAVIS JOHN--10, Effingham Co. (R. Castleberry)--17 Mar 1846--1225 (0.4 Acres)--12--1Cher.
ALLEN JOSEPH--602, Taliaferro Co.--15 July 1834--30 (35.5 Acres)--13S--1Cher.
ROBERTS JAMES--Roberts, Hall Co.--29 March 1836--31 (5.5 Acres)--13S--1Cher.
GRAY MARY wid.--Parhams, Warren Co. (Jas. Cantrell)--8 Sep 1845--32 (13.25 Acres)--13S--1Cher.
TRAP MARTHA widow--Perrys, Baldwin County--8 December 1835--90 (32.5 Acres)--13S--1Cher.
WOOD THOMAS his orphans--Georges, Appling Co.--28 June 1844--91 (4.75 Acres)--13S--1Cher.
ANDERSON JAMES--Cravens, Coweta Co.--16 September 1836--92 (6.5 Acres)--13S--1Cher.
DICKINSON WILEY--Deavours, Habersham County--26 September 1844--148 (30 Acres)--13S--1Cher.
SORROW ELIAS W.--Colleys, Oglethorpe County--17 August 1837--149 (1.5 Acres)--13S--1Cher.
BROOKS FELIX--Taylors, Jones County--24 May 1842--150 (21.5 Acres)--13S--1Cher.
VERDEL PETER--Houstouns, Chatham County--1 July 1843--151 (38 Acres)--13S--1Cher.
SHEPHERD THOMAS J.--15th, Liberty County--13 December 1834--208 (37.5 Acres)--13S--1Cher.
NELSON JAMES F.--249th Walton Co.--John Smith Jr.--27 Dec 1848--209 (1.25 Ac.)--13S--1Cher.
HARVEY EMANUEL--19th, Bryan County--26 January 1834--210 (37.5 Acres)--13S--1Cher.
COOK BEVERLEY C.--190th, Elbert County--29 June 1843--267 (36.75 Acres)--13S--1Cher.
HUGHLEY WILLIAM--175th, Wilkes County--18 May 1836--268 (3.75 Acres)--13S--1Cher.
DURHAM THOMAS his orphans--Butts, Monroe Co.--16 Nov 1840--269 (25.75 Acres)--13S--1Cher.

HARRIS ALSEY J. wid.--Gridens, Morgan Co.--17 Sept 1835--327 (38.75 Acres)--13S--1Cher.

CLINTON WM. P.--Clintons, Campbell Co.--J.A. McClure--17 June 1845--328 (15.25 Acres)--13S--1Cher.

McCALL JOHN--Stones, Irwin County--16 December 1834--329 (8.75 Acres)--13S--1Cher.

BUCHANNAN ISAAC--Deatons, Jackson County--27 August 1835--330 (34.5 Acres)--13S--1Cher.

SCOTT JOSIAH B.--Parks, Walton County--30 June 1834--388 (36.25 Acres)--13S--1Cher.

SMITH HENRY B.--Smiths, Madison County--3 September 1835--389 (1 Acre)--13S--1Cher.

SMITH STEPHEN--Seeys, Hall County--9 September 1836--390 (17.75 Acres)--13S--1Cher.

JORDAN ELIZABETH wid.--Gunns, Jefferson Co.--9 October 1834--451 (35.5 Acres)--13S--1Cher.

GANES COOPER--119th, Richmond Co. (R. Banks)--15 May 1846--452 (1.5 Acres)--13S--1Cher.

SCARBOROUGH PERRIN--73rd, Burke Co.--J. Turner--8 Sept. 1845--453 (3.25 Acres)--13S--1Cher.

HARRIS NATHANIEL--Parks, Walton Co.--12 November 1838--454 (3.5 Acres)--13S--1Cher.

MILLS JOHN B.--Killens, Decatur County--17 December 1835--455 (21 Acres)--13S--1Cher.

KIRK WILLIAM--Hitchcocks, Muscogee County--14 September 1835--518 (37.5 Acres)--13S--1Cher.

GIBBS SAMPSON--Stones, Irwin County--18 December 1835--519 (34 Acres)--13S--1Cher.

HIGGINBOTHAM NELSON--Higginbothams, Madison Co.--2 Oct 1835--520 (20.75 Acres)--13S--1Cher.

RHODES HIRAM B.--Moores, Randolph Co.--8 January 1834--521 (32 Acres)--13S--1Cher.

TYE DANIEL--Harts, Jones County--22 November 1834--32 (35.5 Acres)--13N--1Cher.

HAWKINS BENJAMIN--589th, Upson County--9 June 1834--33 (17.6 Acres)--13N--1Cher.

JENKINS THOMAS--Fulks, Wilkes County--9 June 1834--97 (25.5 Acres)--13N--1Cher.

BURCH CHARLES--124th, Richmond County--9 January 1836--98 (1.2 Acres)--13N--1Cher.

GRIZZEL JAMES--Derings, Henry County--15 September 1835--99 (15 Acres)--13N--1Cher.

DOOLY CLEMENT--Burnetts, Habersham County--22 May 1834--159 (14 Acres)--13N--1Cher.

McCLENDON STEPHEN--364th, Jasper Co.--R. Castleberry--19 Mch 1846--160 (.9 Acre)--13N--1Cher.

SHIPP WILSHIRE L.--Shearrers, Coweta County--19 June 1834--220 (18 Acres)--13N--1Cher.

GUNN JAMES--Gunns, Jones County--2 March 1836--281 (6 Acres)--13N--1Cher.

HOOKS WILLIAM--Whipples, Wilkinson County--16 November 1841--400 (2 Acres)--13N--1Cher.

YARBOROUGH JOHN H.--Bustins, Pike County--21 December 1835--401 (35 Acres)--13N--1Cher.

KNOWLES RICE P.--365th, Jasper Co.--3 December 1836--456 (22 Acres)--13N--1Cher.

McNEES SAMUEL B.--Latimers, DeKalb County--16 June 1836--457 (16 Acres)--13N--1Cher.

JARRETT JAMES--Ridens, Jackson County--23 February 1836--458 (35 Acres)--13N--1Cher.

HOMES ASHBERRY--Prescotts, Twiggs County--17 May 1843--459 (36 Acres)--13N--1Cher.

LANGLY JAMES--Newsoms, Warren County--12 August 1834--516 (38 Acres)--13N--1Cher.

TOMLIN HEZEKIAH W.--Lanes, Morgan County--3 September 1834--517 (26 Acres)--13N--1Cher.

TORNLIN HEZEKIAH W. See Tomlin Hezekiah W.--13N--1Cher.

HORN ISAAC--Brooks, Muscogee County--30 June 1843--548 (2.1 Acres)--13N--1Cher.

LIGHTFOOT JAMES L. his orphans--608th, Taliaferro Co.--Not given--549 (3 Acres)--13N--1Cher.

ETHREDGE ENOC--Haygoods, Washington County--Not given--550 (3.5 Acres)--13N--1Cher.

GUNN LARKIN R.--608th, Taliafero County--Not given--551 (4.5 Acres)--13N--1Cher.

SANDERS DAVID--Latimers, DeKalb County--Not given--552 (6.5 Acres)--13N--1Cher.

NORTON JAMES J. orphan--Fews, Muscogee County--Not given--553 (6.5 Acres)--13N--1Cher.

CARTER JOHN J.--Ricks, Laurens County--Not given--554 (6.5 Acres)--13N--1Cher.

BRADY ALFRED--Groces, Bibb County--Not given--555 (6.5 Acres)--13N--1Cher.

HARRIS ALEXANDER F.--Mullins, Carroll County--Not given--556 (6.5 Acres)--13N--1Cher.

SUTHERLAND JAMES--Bells, Columbia County--Not given--557 (7 Acres)--13N--1Cher.

REED MARY widow--Bustins, Pike County--1 December 1838--558 (7.2 Acres)--13N--1Cher.

BOYKIN HENRY--Hendons, Carroll County--3 December 1842--559 (7.5 Acres)--13N--1Cher.

CALVIN JOHN--271st, McIntosh Co.--J.D. Palmore--12 May 1846--560 (7.5 Acres)--13N--1Cher.

KENDRICK JACOB B.--174th, Wilkes County--4 September 1835--561 (7.5 Acres)--13N--1Cher.

RAGAN MARTHA widow--Killins, Decatur Co.--A. Palmore--8 Sep

1845--562 (7.5 Acres)--13N--1Cher.

STILLMAN SAMUEL--Cokers, Troup County--A. Palmore--8 Sept 1845--563 (7.2 Acres)--13N--1Cher.

DURAN JESSE--Allens, Henry County--J. Talley--17 March 1846--564 (7.2 Acres)--13N--1Cher.

WAMACK WILEY--Whipples, Wilkinson County--1 March 1834--565 (7.2 Acres)--13N--1Cher.

WHEELER WHITE--55th. Emanuel County--Not given--566 (7.2 Acres)--13N--1Cher.

TREDAWAY WILLIAM--Ellis, Rabun County--Not given--567 (7.4 Acres)--13N--1Cher.

WICKER WILEY W.--Perrys, Baldwin County--Not given--568 (8 Acres)--13N--1Cher.

STALY JOHN orphan--11th, Effingham County--17 November 1838--569 (8 Acres)--13N--1Cher.

CHAPPELL OBADIAH--249th, Walton Co.--A. Randolph--4 Nov 1853--570 (6.8 Acres)--13N--1Cher.

BEATY JAMES--Allersons, Walton Co.--19 February 1842--571 (6.6 Acres)--13N--1Cher.

KENDRICK JONES--174th. Wilkes County--9 May 1834--572 (7.7 Acres)--13N--1Cher.

ECKLES THOMAS orphans--168th, Wilkes County--21 December 1836--573 (8 Acres)--13N--1Cher.

BERRY ANDREW J.--Shearers, Coweta County--13 January 1834--574 (8 Acres)--13N--1Cher.

McGIBONEY ERASMUS--144th, Greene Co.--Geo. Keith--6 March 1847--575 (8 Acres)--13N--1Cher.

SKINNER JESSE M. orphan--Heads, Butts County--Not given--576 (8 Acres)--13N--1Cher.

VARDEMAN WILLIAM--Tuggles, Meriwether Co.--G. Keith--17 Mar 1846--577 (8 Acres)--13N--1Cher.

FEARS EZEKIEL--294th. Jasper County--24 March 1836--578 (3.6 Acres)--13N--1Cher.

ALLMAND JOHN--Hoods, Henry County--21 January 1836--579 (9 Acres)--13N--1Cher.

AYRES LARKIN C.--Mangums, Franklin County--24 September 1835--580 (34 Acres)--13N--1Cher.

HEFLIN JOHNSON--Smiths, Henry County--13 December 1837--581 (18 Acres)--13N--1Cher.

MILLER SOLOMON--112th, Hancock County--8 December 1835--582 (7 Acres)--13N--1Cher.

BOWER JONATHAN--25th, Glynn County--16 June 1835--583 (12 Acres)--13N--1Cher.

DWELE LEMUEL--600th, Richmond County--25 February 1836--584 (16 Acres)--13N--1Cher.

CASEY PARRIS P.--Martins, Hall County--5 July 1834--585 (2 Acres)--13N--1Cher.

WIGGINS JOHN--Lamberths, Fayette County--9 June 1834--586 (14.9 Acres)--13N--1Cher.

GUESS WILLIAM--Ogdens, Camden County--19 January 1835--58--14--1Cher.

PRATOR JOHN D.--470th, Upson County--31 January 1835--59--14--1Cher.

EVANS ARDEN his orphans--Hemphills, Morgan County--1 July 1843--60--14--1Cher.

HAMLET SANDERS W.--Maguires, Morgan County--6 December 1835--61--14--1Cher.

EDWARDS ALFRED SR.--Johnsons, DeKalb County--20 March 1835--62--14--1Cher.

SWAR JOHN L.--121st, Richmond County--15 May 1834--63--14--1Cher.

SMAR JOHN L. See Swar John L.--14--1Cher.

LAMAR JOHN L. See Swar John L.--14--1Cher.

PATTERSON ALEXANDER--Whipples, Wilkinson County--5 April 1834--64--14--1Cher.

JONES JAMES H. JR.--102nd, Hancock County--29 March 1834--170 (40 Acres)--14--1Cher.

BAKER DENNIS B.--417th, Walton County--5 April 1834--171--14--1Cher.

MARTIN CATHERINE widow--Candlers, Bibb County--5 April 1834--172--14--1Cher.

McCALL ROBERT--Folsoms, Lowndes County--10 December 1834--173--14--1Cher.

BARTON ALLEN--McMillons, Lincoln County--S.W. Lee--9 May 1846--174--14--1Cher.

ELLIS WILLIAM--Fryers, Telfair County--25 November 1842--175 (22.5 Acres)--14--1Cher.

WALKER EZEKIEL--Halls, Butts County--15 December 1834--176--14--1Cher.

FEW IGNATIOUS A. SR.--Fews, Muscogee County--16 February 1834--274--14--1Cher.

SANDERS AUGUSTUS M.--Murphys, Columbia County--1 June 1843--275--14--1Cher.

BELCHER PHILIP--Alexanders, Jefferson County--7 November 1839--276--14--1Cher.

WARD THOMAS--Belchers, Jasper County--22 July 1839--277--14--1Cher.

BROWNING EDMOND--McCLAINS, Newton County--15 May 1837--278--14--1Cher.

BATTLE JOSEPH A.--602nd, Taliaferro Co.--W.B. Parker--20 February 1846--371--14--1Cher.

CALDWELL WHITFIELD--Stricklands, Meriwether County--29 December 1838--372--14--1Cher.

DOUGLASS JOHN--Cherokee Hill, Chatham Co.--6 February 1835--462--14--1Cher.

ELLIOTT WILLIAM--Covingtons, Pike County--20 April 1835--463--

14--1Cher.

MANNER HENRY--Morgans, Madison County--2 April 1836--464--14--1Cher.

THWEATT KINCHEN P.--Also brooks, Jones Co.--E. Thomas--17 Nov 42 & 9 Feb 46--465--14--1Cher.

PEEK ROBERT JR.--Harris, Greene County--7 August 1834--466--14--1Cher.

BRADBURG JOSEPH--Smiths, Campbell County--29 March 1834--467--14--1Cher.

CORREY THOMAS--320th, Baldwin County--8 November 1836--548--14--1Cher.

KIGHT DAVID--Robinsons, Fayette County--29 March 1834--549--14--1Cher.

BOISCLAIR LEWIS A.L.--120th, Richmond County--7 April 1837--550--14--1Cher.

NEIL MAC REA--Morrisons, Montgomery County--21 February 1837--551--14--1Cher.

SPRING JAMES--McCoys, Houston County--20 January 1837--552--14--1Cher.

CAWTHEN SAMUEL--Duprees, Morgan County--12 February 1836--553--14--1Cher.

GIBSON SAMUEL--McClains, Newton County--10 December 1835--630--14--1Cher.

WALKER ALLEN A.--Garners, Washington Co.--C. Day--11 May 1846--707--14--1Cher.

CHASTAIN JONATHAN D.--Jones, Habersham County--28 November 1835--708--14--1Cher.

SAILERS JAMES--McGinnis, Jackson County--25 July 1834--783--14--1Cher.

TUCKER WILLIAM--Wilsons, Jasper County--Not given--784--14--1Cher.

SANFORD JESSE--Dyers, Habersham County--10 December 1835--785--14--1Cher.

HICKS SAMUEL--Crows, Pike County--11 December 1834--862--14--1Cher.

CHASTAIN JOHN--Chastains, Habersham County--17 February 1834--939--14--1Cher.

DOUGLASS JOHN--Cherokee Hill, Chatham County--20 December 1834--940--14--1Cher.

BIRD GEORGE L.--604th, Taliaferro County--2 December 1836--941--14--1Cher.

MILLER PRESTON--Griffins, Hall County--19 December 1835--942--14--1Cher.

EVERETT JAMES A.--Marshalls, Crawford County--19 December 1835--1017--14--1Cher.

DABONVILLE, JOSEPH--McIntosh County--1 July 1843--1018--14--1Cher.

OGLETREE PHILAMON--Parhams, Harris County--28 March 1836--1019--14--1Cher.

SHEPHERD MARY ANN W. widow--Gittens, Fayette County--27 November 1835--1096--14--1Cher.

LEVERETT JESSE--Williams, Jasper County--27 November 1835--1097--14--1Cher.

BENNETT CHRISTOPHER G.--8th, Chatham County--8 December 1834--1098--14--1Cher.

ANTHONY MICAJAH T.--Moseleys, Wilkes County--1 December 1835--1169--14--1Cher.

SMITH SAMUEL--Robinsons, Harris County--10 December 1834--1170--14--1Cher.

TARROW DAVID--Whelches, Habersham County--10 December 1834--1171--14--1Cher.

BYNUM REASON--Smiths, Houston County--24 May 1837--1172--14--1Cher.

NORRIS ARCHER--Smiths, Madison County--16 August 1834--1173--14--1Cher.

McDONALD A.H.--Jordans, Harris County--20 July 1844--1238--14--2Cher.

DYAL LYLPHIE widow--24th, McIntosh County--1 July 1843--1239--14--1Cher.

SKINNER JONATHAN--Roes, Burke County--7 June 1834--1241--14--1Cher.

HENDERSON SAMUEL R.--Ridens, Jackson Co.--W.C. Carr--10 September 1845--1242--14--1Cher.

TOWNSEND THOMAS SR.--Fields, Habersham County--25 February 1834--1243--14--1Cher.

KINDRICK SYLVANUS--Kindricks, Monroe County--25 February 1834--1299--14--1Cher.

HOLDEN THOMAS--602nd, Taliaferro County--25 February 1834--1300--14--1Cher.

AVERY JONATHAN--Edwards, Talbot County--1 July 1843--1301--14--1Cher.

KEENER HENRY--122nd, Richmond County--7 June 1834--1302--14--1Cher.

JONES DAVID G.--Hobkerks, Camden County--19 July 1834--1303--14--1Cher.

AKINS CATLETT J.--Robinsons, Harris County--25 February 1834--1304--14--1Cher.

POWELL WILLIAM his orphans--Streetmans, Twiggs County--24 February 1835--1332--14--1Cher.

FELTON HARTWELL--4th Section, Cherokee County--5 November 1834--1358--14--1Cher.

TURNER THOMAS SR.--374th, Putnam County--21 December 1842--1359--14--1Cher.

ALEXANDER JAMES S.--Flemmings, Franklin County--25 February 1834--1360--14--1Cher.

CONNER, JOHN--McEwins, Monroe County--27 December 1834--1361--14--1Cher.

LANGSTON WILLIAM--Baughs, Jackson County--28 May 1835--1362--14--1Cher.

BRACKETT JOHN--Lamberths, Fayette County--25 February 1834--1363--14--1Cher.

WHIGHAM JOHN W.--Hannahs, Jefferson County--25 January 1837--1364--14--1Cher.

RICKETSON BENJAMIN SR.--Parhams, Warren County--16 March 1838--1365--14--1Cher.

COPE ADAM--Sanderlins, Chatham County--26 November 1834--1366--14--1Cher.

WADE JAMES--Smiths, Franklin County--25 February 1834--1367--14--1Cher.

STANFORD MARGARET widow--588th, Upson County--24 February 1843--1378--14--1Cher.

HOLMES JAMES P.--458th, Early County--Geo. Kellogg--20 November 1845--14--1Cher.

WILLIAMS JOHN convict & sailor--320th, Bald. Co.--Saml. Patterson--9/8/45--1380--14--1Cher.

MITCHELL WILLIAM--Cleghorns, Madison County--26 November 1838--1381--14--1Cher.

BOYD GEORGE--Jacks, Clarke County--4 December 1834--1382--14--1Cher.

SAILORS WILLIAM--Jones, Madison County--11 April 1834--1383--14--1Cher.

MOON ARCHELAUS--Smiths, Madison County--7 May 1839--1384--14--1Cher.

SANDIFORD THOMAS R.--Olivers, Twiggs County--5 June 1843--1385--14--1Cher.

TURNER DANIEL--Sumerlins, Bulloch County--18 December 1835--1386--14--1Cher.

PARKER WILLIAM H.--Bowers, Elbert County--1 July 1843--1387--14--1Cher.

WATSON JOSEPH--Chambers, Gwinnett County--5 November 1839--1388--14--1Cher.

BRANHAM WILEY--374th, Putnam County--8 November 1839--1389--14--1Cher.

TOMLIN ASARIAH--Martins, Newton County--25 February 1834--1395--14--1Cher.

BILLINGSLEA JAMES F.--Maguires, Morgan County--22 August 1837--1396--14--1Cher.

GAZEAWAY JOHN--Wynns, Gwinnett County--1 December 1835--1397--14--1Cher.

GRACE JOHN--555th, Upson County--4 May 1841--1401--14--1Cher.

PRICKET JOSIAH--Daniels, Hall County--8 May 1838--1402--14--1Cher.

WHITE JOHN--Chambers, Gwinnett County--25 September 1835--1403--14--1Cher.

BARKSDALE JOHN--Brooks, Muscogee County--5 November 1834--1407--14--1Cher.

STRICKLAND JOHN S.--Morgans, Appling County--21 November 1835--1408--14--1Cher.

SOWELL FRANCIS--Clelands, Chatham County--26 December 1842--1410--14--1Cher.

DIMON WILLIAM T.--Kellums, Talbot County--1 July 1843--1411--14--1Cher.

MARSHALL MATHEW T.--Simmons, Crawford County--4 December 1839--1412--14--1Cher.

MILES WILLIAM--Gittens, Fayette County--13 March 1835--1413--14--1Cher.

BRAMBLET JOHN--Dobbs, Hall County--27 January 1834--1414--14--1Cher.

JORDAN WILLIAM D.--Lightfoots, Washington County--12 May 1834--1415--14--1Cher.

HULL THOMAS SR.--Heads, Butts County--8 May 18??--1416--14--1Cher.

McGEHEE CRAWFORD--Sims, Troup County--25 February 1836?--1417--14--1Cher.

FINLEY ALLEN--Tuggles, Meriwether County--11 November 1840--19--15--1Cher.

SMITH HENRY SR.--Covingtons, Pike County (T.L. Brown)--20 May 1846--20--15--1Cher.

RUTHERFORD WILLIAM--Barkers, Gwinnett County--C. Day--11 May 1846--21--15--1Cher.

BARNETT WILLIAM--Murpheys, Columbia County--1 July 1843--34--15--1Cher.

COWEN ROBERT--Nesbits, Newton County--1 July 1843--35--15--1Cher.

WILDER ELIZA S. "orph F.K.J.W."--34th, Scriven County--Not given --48--15--1Cher.

DUGAS VINCENDIEVE--122nd, Richmond County--7 June 1843--49--15--1Cher.

BROOKS ISHAM--Cokers, Troup County--5 March 1836--62--15--1Cher.

MORRIS MARY widow--295th, Jasper County--1 July 1843--63--15--1Cher.

WEIR JOHN S.--Hearns, Butts County--1 July 1843--76--15--1Cher.

RAGSDALE ELIJAH--Hutsons, Newton County--6 November 1840--77--15--1Cher.

PATE THOMAS--Martins, Stewart County--6 July 1840--89--15--1Cher.

ELSBERRY LINDSEY--Gillis, DeKalb County--8 November 1838--90--15--1Cher.

STEPHENS ALLEN--Dyers, Habersham County--S.G. Day--12 May 1846--91--15--1Cher.

KERBY ARTHUR SR.--Slaters, Bulloch County--20 April 1839--102--15--1Cher.

OCONNOR PATRICK B.--295th, Jasper County--L.W. Cooper--21 November 1853--103--15--1Cher.

BATTS WILLIAM--Carswells, Jefferson Co.--A.J. & D.W. Orr--16 Feb. 1846--104--15--1Cher.

BARTLEMAN JOHN W.--Robinsons, Putnam County--S.G. Day--12 May 1846--118--15--1Cher.

HENDRY ANN widow--Bakers, Liberty County--29 March 1836--119--15--1Cher.

OLIVER SAMUEL--Hutsons, Newton County--S.G. Day--12 May 1846--120--15--1Cher.

MOON ANN AMELIA widow--398th, Richmond County--Not given--121--15--1Cher.

SWEARINGEN BENJAMIN H.--585th, Dooly County--19 February 1834--122--15--1Cher.

FORD MARIAM--Everetts, Washington County--30 January 1834--141--15--1Cher.

WATERS HENRY--Seays, Hall County--6 March 1837--142--15--1Cher.

SHELMAN THOMAS P.C.--Williams, Decatur County--31 March 1834--161--15--1Cher.

HILL WAID--Robinsons, Putnam County--6 February 1834--162--15--1Cher.

EDMUNDSON JAMES SR.--Barkers, Gwinnett County--19 January 1834--181--15--1Cher.

HAMBY WILLIAM SR.--Hensons, Rabun County--J.A. Sands--21 May 1846--182--15--1Cher.

TORRANCE JAMES--75th, Burke County--26 November 1836--183--15--1Cher.

GALLAWAY JOHN--Allens, Monroe County--19 November 1836--199--15--1Cher.

CHRISTIAN GIDEON--Tuggles, Meriwether County--Not given--200--15--1Cher.

WILLIAMS HENRY H.--Says, DeKalb County--Not given--201--15--1Cher.

YOUNG MICHAEL--Sam Streetmans, Twiggs County--19 February 1834--202--15--1Cher.

GIBSON NELSON--Thompsons, Henry County--30 November 1838--219--15--1Cher.

NARRAMORE ELIE W.--Griffins, Hall County--8 December 1841--220--15--1Cher.

WAMMACK WILLIAM--Phillips, Jasper County--W.B. Parker--20 February 1846--237--15--1Cher.

CHARLTON THOMAS U.P.--Valleaus, Chatham Co.--W.B. Parker--20 Feb. 1846--238--15--1Cher.

MARTIN JAMES--Brocks, Habersham Co.--W.B. Parker--20 Feb. 1846--254--15--1Cher.

SHELL GREEN--103rd, Hancock County--21 December 1842--255--15--1Cher.

CHITWOOD PLEASANT--Chambers, Gwinnett County--27 January 1834--256--15--1Cher.

WHITE DANIEL--588th, Upson County--J.A. Sands--21 May 1846--272--15--1Cher.

TURNER JAMES--Wallis, Irwin County--19 February 1834--273--15--1Cher.

TAYLOR SUSANNAH widow--Taylors, Elbert County--21 June 1843--274--15--1Cher.

BOHANNAN BUDDA--454th, Walton County--13 December 1842--291--15--1Cher.

HATHCOCK MIDDLETON--Hammonds, Franklin County--24 March 1837--15--1Cher.

BRIDGES HOWELL--Simmonds, Crawford County--W.B. Parker--20 Feb. 1846--293--15--1Cher.

HINES HOWELL--10th, Effingham Co.--A.J. & D.W. Orr--24 February 1846--308--15--1Cher.

SANDERLIN JESSE--1st, Chatham County--Not given--309--15--1Cher.

RAINWATER ABNER--106th, Hancock County--1 July 1843--310--15--1Cher.

HOWELL ISAAC--Neals, Campbell County--J. Baldwin--7 July 1846--311--15--1Cher.

GRIFFIN JOHN--Whitakers, Crawford County--Chs. Day--10 Feb. 1846--327--15--1Cher.

HUCKABY JAMES--Roberts, Hall County (T.R. Bloom)--9 February 1846--328--15--1Cher.

WHEELER JOHN W.--Neals, Campbell County (Chs. Day)--10 February 1846--329--15--1Cher.

MAYFIELD OBADIAH--Thomas, Clarke County--27 March 1834--330--15--1Cher.

HARPER GEORGE--Bensons, Lincoln County--27 June 1843--352--15--1Cher.

ARNOLD JOHN--Olivers, Twiggs County--17 May 1841--353--15--1Cher.

HARRIS NATHAN--Whitakers, Crawford County--F. Logan--12 September 1845--354--15--1Cher.

HORISE NATHAN See Harris Nathan--15--1Cher.

BRITT HENRY--Britts, Randolph County--F. Logan--12 September 1845--15--1Cher.

HAIL JOHN--454th, Walton County--1 December 1836--380--15--1Cher.

FINDLEY WILLIAM--Griffins, Emanuel County--Ira R. Foster--27 Nov. 1847--381--15--1Cher.

WARREN WILLIAM--Mitchells, Jackson County--19 September 1842--382--15--1Cher.

SUMMERTIN THOMAS orph--Jones, Morgan County--Not given--410--15--1Cher.

HARDMAN ALLEN--Latimers, DeKalb County--14 December 1836--411-15--1Cher.

SIMMONS WILLIAM P.--Lesters, Monroe County--H. Willingham--12 May 1846--412--15--1Cher.

REEVES JOHN--Johnsons, DeKalb County--16 December 1840--413--15--1Cher.

WHITE CYRUS--Williams, Jasper County--29 November 1839--445--15--1Cher.

GORDON ALEXANDER J.--Currys, Meriwether County--23 June 1834--446--15--1Cher.

MCMATH PHILLIP--Newmans, Thomas County--7 December 1836--447--15--1Cher.

FULLER BENJAMIN F.--Wootens, Monroe County--30 June 1843--475--15--1Cher.

BAKER JOHN M.C.L.--McClelands, Irwin County--8 March 1837--476--15--1Cher.

BENTLEY JOHN--Heads, Jones County--L. Brown--12 May 1846--477--15--1Cher.

CANNON ELIZABETH widow--121st, Richmond Co.--F. Logan--12 Sept. 1845--478--15--1Cher.

BAKER HUGH--Latimers, DeKalb County--F. Logan--12 September 1845--479--15--1Cher.

POWELL JOHN--Martins, Washington County--1 July 1843--496--15--1Cher.

SHIELDS JAMES--Murphys, Columbia County--21 November 1837--497--15--1Cher.

ROWLES JESSE--Madens, Pike County--W.B. Parker--20 February 1846--498--15--1Cher.

LAMAR EZEKIEL--McMillens, Lincoln County--18 December 1838--501--15--1Cher.

SMITH GRIFFIN H.--Whipples, Wilkinson County--Not given--502--15--1Cher.

BOWEN NANCY widow--Clarks, Morgan County--1 July 1843--503--15--1Cher.

CRAWFORD CHARLES--Groces, Bibb County--J.N. Smith--1 October 1846--504--15--1Cher.

OWEN WILLIAM B.--Wilsons, Pike County--Not given--505--15--1Cher.

MILES ELIJAH SR.--672nd, Harris County--12 June 1843--506--15--1Cher.

ALLEN WILLIAM H.--Allens, Bibb County--4 August 1835--507--15--1Cher.

WILKINS JOHN--Sanderlins, Chatham County--W.T. Hansell--20 May 1846--508--16--1Cher.

HENDRIX JOHN--35th, Scriven County--30 June 1843--509--15--1Cher.

LEVINGSTON THOMAS--693rd, Heard County, 2 July 1835--516--15--1Cher.

CRUMPTON THOMAS--Woodruffs, Campbell County--1 March 1834--517--15--1Cher.

HOLMES SHARICK--Kellys, Elbert County--30 November 1839--518--15--1Cher.

LIVINGSTON THOMAS See Levingston Thomas--15--1Cher.

STEWART THOMAS S.--34th, Scriven County--W.B. Parker--20 February 1846--519--15--1Cher.

WHITE MILLER H.--470th, Upson County--27 September 1842--520--15--1Cher.

BREWER ELIZABETH widow//Lunsford, Elbert Co.--Thos. Mitchell--20 May 1846--521--15--1Cher.

MOULTRIE JOSEPH J. revd.--121st, Richmond County--Not given--522--15--1Cher.

HAN ICHABOD--Boyntons, Twiggs County--1 July 1843--524--15--1Cher.

WILLIAMS HIRAM--Parks, Walton County--23 December 1834--525--15--1Cher.

FURLOW OSBORN S.--143rd, Green County--21 December 1838--526--15--1Cher.

STEPHENS MILES--McKorkles, Jasper County--10 February 1834--527--15--1Cher.

GAINS ANN T. widow--Brews, Monroe County--21 December 1838--528--15--1Cher.

McLEROY NATHAN--672nd, Harris County--21 December 1838--529--15--1Cher.

WIGGINS WILLIS--McCullers, Newton County--J.A. Sands--21 May 1846--530--15--1Cher.

HAWKINS EDWARD--374th, Putnam County--9 March 1836--1--1--2Cher.

MENZIES ARCHIBALD--Witherspoons, Jackson County--16 June 1835--76--1--2Cher.

THRASH VOLUNTINE--656th, Troup County--4 May 1835--77--1--2Cher.

TANNER WILLIAM H.--Hearns, Butts County--23 December 1836--78--1--2Cher.

NORTH MARCUS D.--Wares, Coweta County--16 November 1835--79--1--2Cher.

STEPHENS OLIVER--McKorkles, Jasper County--11 December 1834--149--1--2Cher.

EDMONSON DANIEL--Suttons, Habersham County--16 May 1837--150--1--2Cher.

WILLIAMS JAMES--174th, Wilkes County--Wm. F. Groves--23 February 1846--151--1--2Cher.

WAGGONER GEORGE B.--Griers, Warren County--3 May 1836--152--1--2Cher.

McGRAW JOSEPH--Allens, Bibb County--16 December 1835--218--1--2Cher.

JONES JESSE--Keeners, Rabun County--7 June 1843--219--1--2Cher.

TURNER MICAJAH--Hughes, Habersham County--12 December 1834--220--1--2Cher.

PARKER L. PARKER--Mayos, Wilkinson County--T.R. Bloom--13 September 1845--279--1--2Cher.

STATIGERY JOHN F. widower--3rd, Chatham County--12 December 1834--282--1--2Cher.

BIFFLE JOHN--Givvins, DeKalb County--1 July 1843--283--1--2Cher.

FEATHERSTON WILLIAM--Rhodes, DeKalb County--J.C. Johnson--20 May 1846--284--1--2Cher.

YORK WILLIAM--Blackstocks, Hall County--14 March 1834--285--1--2Cher.

MAY WILLIAM--Nichols, Fayette County--14 November 1836--286--1--2Cher.

CASSEL JAMES--Woodruffs, Campbell County--1 June 1843--287--1--2Cher.

RALSTON DAVID--Hearndons, Hall County--25 November 1840--288--1--2Cher.

SELF JOHN N.--Chastains, Habersham County--27 December 1836--292--1--2Cher.

HILL ROBERT H. his orphans--Hills, Baldwin County--Not given--293--1--2Cher.

REEVES JAMES H.--Gays, Harris County--B.H. Moultrie--19 May 1846--294--1--2Cher.

BRASWELL BENJAMIN--589th, Upson County--15 February 1838--295--1--2Cher.

NISBET JAMES--Ballards, Morgan County--25 June 1838--335--1--2Cher.

WHITFIELD WILLIAM C.--732nd, Dooly County--21 October 1837--336--1--2Cher.

HARDEN JAMES his orphans--Groces, Bibb County--5 November 1840--337--1--2Cher.

KEITH ASA--Chastains, Habersham County--T.R. Bloom--13 September 1845--338--1--2Cher.

SHANNON MARIAH L. orphan--119th, Richmond County--12 October 1837--339--1--2Cher.

SHANNON PETER J. orphan--119th, Richmond County--12 October 1837--339--1--2Cher.

SHANNON GEO. M.W. orphan--119th, Richmond County--12 October 1837--339--1--2Cher.

BONDURANT JOSIAH--Lays, Jackson County--13 November 1838--339--1--2Cher.

BLAKEY DAVID SR.--105th, Baldwin County--T. Cherry--9 February 1846--379--1--2Cher.

BINION WILEY H.--Murpheys, Columbia County--1 July 1843--380--1--2Cher.

PAGE JESSE his orphans--Mitchells, Marion County--1 July 1843--380--1--2Cher.

COX WILEY J.--362nd, Jasper County--1 July 1843--419--1--2Cher.

TRANNAN GEORGE W.--Allens, Campbell County--3 January 1834--420--1--2Cher.

SMALLWOOD ELIJAH--Harts, Jones County--3 November 1835--457--1--2Cher.

McCANE THOMAS U.T.--735th, Troup County--3 November 1835--458--1--2Cher.

SAMPLE CATHERINE J. orphan--Taylors, Putnam County--11 January 1836--494--1--2Cher.

BOLER GEORGE his orphans--Graves, Lincoln County--11 January 1836--495--1--2Cher.

BUCKNER HENRY M.--Norris, Monroe County--25 June 1835--496--1--2Cher.

BRAZEEL WARREN H.--168th, Wilkes County--24 July 1834--497--1--2Cher.

GREEN ROGER--Deatons, Jackson County--23 November 1838--530--1--2Cher.

STRANGE BENJAMIN--785th, Sumter County--13 November 1835--531--1--2Cher.

D'LYON MORDECAIE S.--Valleaus, Chatham County--26 November 1834--532--1--2Cher.

CAMP JOHN--Youngs, Carroll County--31 January 1834--533--1--2Cher.

ARNOLD ELIZABETH widow--Guices, Oglethorpe County--9 July 1834--571--1--2Cher.

KERNODLE WILLIAM--Lanes, Morgan County--3 July 1837--572--1--2Cher.

HARRISON GEORGE--Barefields, Jones County--17 November 1838--573--1--2Cher.

SLATTER TALIAFERRO B.--Sparks, Washington Co.--M. Collins--7 July 1846--574--1--2Cher.

BRYAN JOHN--Towers, Gwinnett County--10 February 1834--575--1--2Cher.

MILLER WILLIAM--Herndons, Hall County--10 November 1834--622--1--2Cher.

HALL WILLIAM--Thompsons, Henry County--2 January 1834--623--1--2Cher.

WHORTON ISAAC--1st Section, Cherokee County--18 December 1834--670--1--2Cher.

BUSTIN WILLIAM--Bustins, Pike County--21 July 1835--671--1--2Cher.

HAGAN ISOM--Candlers, Bibb County--29 December 1837--672--1--2Cher.

PLUMMER EDWARD--Maguries, Gwinnett County--15 December 1835--717--1--2Cher.

GODWIN ALEXANDER--720th, Decatur County--J.C. Johnson--20 May 1846--718--1--2Cher.

BAILEY JULIAN--McCullers, Newton County--J.C. Johnson--20 May 1846--719--1--2Cher.

PERDUE NEWTON--Youngs, Jefferson County--28 July 1836--720--1--2Cher.

CONNER ZEPHANIAH F.--Elsworth, Bibb County--3 November 1835--721--1--2Cher.

CHAMBERS WILSON--Currys, Wilkinson County--B.H. Moultrie--19 May 1846--722--1--2Cher.

ARNOLD WESLEY--Shearers, Cowetta County--27 February 1834--723--1--2Cher.

GRIFFITH HENRY W.--Newbys, Jones County--1 July 1843--725--1--2Chers.

JEFFRIES DREWRY--R. Browns, Habersham County--27 February 1834--775--1--2Chers.

PERRY PETER his orphans--Carpenters, Tattnall County--Not given--776--1--2Cher.

WILLIAMS WILLIAM--Bosticks, Twiggs County--15 July 1834--777--1--2Cher.

SOUTHMAYD ANDREW--Mullins, Carroll County--22 December 1838--827--1--2Cher.

HARRINGTON MOSES--Hitchcocks, Muscogee County--S. Riley--20 May 1846--828--1--2Cher.

ONEAL WOOTTEN of Greene County--608th, Taliaferro Co.--3 September 1835--829--1--2Cher.

BOULS NELSON--Currys, Meriwether County--25 November 1834--830--1--2Cher.

KING ISAAC W.--Maddens, Pike County--16 December 1834--881--1--2Cher.

McMULLAN SINCLAIR--561st, Upson County--1 December 1838--882--1--2Cher.

EDWARDS ROBERT L.--Liddles, Jackson County--16 December 1834--883--1--2Cher.

MONK MALONE--Gauldings, Lowndes County--15 December 1838--932--1--2Cher.

PRICHETT WILLIAM H.--294th, Jasper County--Spenser Riley--933--1--2Cher.

HILL GREEN B.--Belchers, Jasper County--27 May 1834--934--1--2Cher.

CAMAK JAMES--320th, Baldwin County--2 April 1836--935--1--2Cher.

EVANS JESSE JR.--606th, Taliaferro County--14 December 1833--936--1--2Cher.

STARLING WILLIAM--Sparks, Washington County--8 March 1834--334--1--2Cher.

McLAUGHLIN GERRARD--120th, Richmond County--C. Day--9 May 1846--1261--16--2Cher.

McCLENDON FRANCIS--Normans, Wilkes Co.--J.U. Horne--12 February 1846--1262--16--2Cher.

PORTER JOHN--430th, Early County--22 November 1837--1263--16--2Cher.

BAUGHN HILLIARD H.--Tuggles, Meriwether Co.--W.B. Johnston--9 May 1846--1264--16--2Cher.

GROVES JOHN W.--Morgans, Madison County--7 November 1839--1265--16--2Cher.

LOUGHRIDGE BENJAMIN--Edwards, Franklin County--27 September 1844--1266--16--2Cher.

WYATT THOMAS--Clarks, Morgan County--15 December 1837--1267--16--2Cher.

BATES NEPOLEON B.--Flynns, Muscogee County--5 September 1837--1268--16--2Cher.

HERNDON BENJAMIN--Woodruffs, Campbell County--21 November 1836--1269--16--2Cher.

DUBERRY THOMAS--Bustins, Pike County--J.U. Horne--12 February 1846--1270--16--2Cher.

GRAINGER JOHN D.--Parks, Walton County--18 February 1839--1271--16--2Cher.

GARRETT JOHN--113th, Hancock County--Harris & Miller--30 October 1845--1272--16--2Cher.

SMITH RANSOM--Bourqouins, Chatham Co.--Timothy Jones--8 November 1845--1273--16--2Cher.

MANIER JESSE--Petersons, Burke County--20 December 1842--1274--16--2Cher.

EASTES SARAH widow--Morris, Crawford County--1 July 1843--1275--16--2Cher.

KIRKLAND JOHN S.--49th, Emanuel County--17 December 1835--1276--16--2Cher.

BENJAMIN MARGARET widow--Bourquins, Chatham Co.--J.U. Horne--12 Feb. 1846--1277--16--2Cher.

MITCHELL ROLAND--Royersters, Franklin County--13 December 1838--1278--16--2Cher.

NICHOLS WILLIAM--Garners, Washington County--19 March 1840--1279--16--2Cher.

GREER ROBERT--Pearces, Houston County--19 December 1837--1280--16--2Cher.

JOHNSON DAVID--Whipples, Wilkinson County--29 June 1839--1281--16--2Cher.

CARIEE JOHN--398th, Richmond County--13 May 1839--1282--16--2Cher.

POSEY WILLIAM--Houses, Henry County--9 December 1835--1283--16--2Cher.

RUNNELS SARAH T. widow--Luncefords, Wilkes County--9 April 1838--1284--16--2Cher.

OLLIFF JOHN--Sumerlins, Bulloch County--18 December 1840--1285--16--2Cher.

WASHINGTON MARTHA widow--Culbreaths, Columbia County--27 November 1838--1286--16--2Cher.

BROWNING YOUNG H.--Griffins, DeKalb County--4 February 1836--1287--16--2Cher.

SANDERS AMBROSE--Bosticks, Twiggs County--13 August 1839--1288--16--2Cher.

ANDERSON GEORGE T.--Youngs, Carroll County--24 June 1834--1289--16--2Cher.

MARTIN JOHN his orphans--Seays, Hall County--30 April 1838--1290--16--2Cher.

RAHN JOHNATHAN--11th, Effingham County--3 December 1836--1291--16--2Cher.

STANFILL RAHN--Edwards, Montgomery County--24 April 1840--1292--16--2Cher.

DUNAGAN JOSHUA--Herndons, Hall County--30 January 1838--1293--16--2Cher.

POTTS WILLIAM E.--Kindricks, Monroe County--21 January 1835--1294--16--2Cher.

WAKEFIELD SAMUEL--Shearers, Coweta County--1 February 1836--1295--16--2Cher.

McCLAIN EPHRAIM--McClains, Rabun County--12 September 1834--1296--16--2Cher.

THOMPSON DANIEL--48th, Emanuel County--16 April 1834--757--17--2Cher.

ADCOCK ANDERSON W.--Walkers, Harris County--8 December 1834--17--2Cher.

BRASWELL BLANEY--Durhams, Talbot County--22 April 1836--828--17--2Cher.

RIGANS MARY widow--Waldens, Pulaski County--1 October --------829--17--2Cher.

PEARSON JEREMIAH--Jordans, Harris County--10 July 1834--830--17--2Cher.

McLENDON JOEL--Burks, Stewart County--11 November 1837--896--17--2Cher.

JOHNSON DARIUS--656th, Troup County--25 March 1836--897--17--2Chers.

MORRIS WILLIAM G.--Griffins, Hall County--17 November 1837--898--17--2Cher.

TUGGLE JOHN JUNR.--Trouts, Hall County--24 November 1836--963--17--2Cher.

HARY WILLIAM--Allens, Henry County--25 April 1834--964--17--2Cher.

DAVIS GARDNER H.--Mizells, Talbot County--30 March 1837--966--17--2Cher.

DAVIDSON JAMES--Streetmans, Twiggs County--29 August 1834--967--17--2Cher.

SHACKLEFORD JOSEPH H.--Taylors, Elbert County--29 Nov. 1834--gr. as 960--968--17--2Cher.

WISDOM ELLENOR widow--366th, Jasper County--20 January 1837--969--17--2Cher.

FLEMMING ROBERT--Flemmings, Franklin County--21 Jan. 1836--970--17--2Cher.

COCKRAM JAMES--Fields, Habersham County--5 Jan. 1834--971--17--2Cher.

BROWN WILLIAM--Hattons, Baker County--14 Sept. 1835--972--17--2Cher.

MILLER ELI--Wagnons, Carrol County--17 December 1834--1017--17--2Cher.

HEAD JAMES A.--Martins, Hall County--23 November 1836--1018--17--2Cher.

ANDREWS GARNETT--Moseleys, Wilkes County--3 February 1837--1019--17--2Cher.

NASH JAMES C. JUNR.--394th, Montgomery County--3 Dec. 1834--1020--17--2Cher.

WILKINS DAVID--Thompsons, Henry County--17 December 1833--1021--17--2Cher.

SNEAD ROBERT R.--8th, Chatham County--16 June 1834--1022--17--2Cher.

SPENCE LUCRETIA widow--Clelands, Chatham County--27 October 1834--1023--17--2Cher.

HARGROVES GEORGE SR.--Fews, Muscogee County--13 November 1838--1024--17--2Cher.

STEWART ELI A.--Gunns, Jefferson County--28 December 1835--1025--17--2Cher.

STRONG SHEROD his orps.--Higginbothams, Carroll County--24 August 1854--1034--17--2Cher.

BROWN HUGH--Deavours, Habersham County--11 December 1834--1035--17--2Cher.

CAMPBELL CHARTER--Ballards, Morgan County--13 November 1834--1053--17--2Cher.

PITTMAN MARTIN H.--Ridens, Jackson County--W.A. Carr--20 May 1846--1054--17--2Cher.

ALLEN JAMES L.--Stephens, Habersham County--22 December 1834--17--2Cher.

McCLUNG WILLIAM W.--Reids, Gwinnett County--28 February 1834--1056--17--2Cher.

PARHAM ELIJAH--Parhams, Warren County--W.S. Thompson--13 September 1835--1058--17--2Cher.

JOHNSON WILLIAM--Smiths, Henry County--W.S. Thompson--13 September 1835--1059--17--2Cher.

BOSTWICK CHARLES H.--McCullers, Newton Co.--(W.S. Thompson)--13 September 1834--1060--17--2Cher.

SMITH JOHN G.--Blounts, Wilkinson County--2 January 1840--1061--17--2Chers.

KING SARAH widow--Buck Branch, Clarke County--1 July 1843--1062--17--2Cher.

HAYMANS ELISHA--Bryants, Burke County--19 December 1836--1063--17--2Cher.

ELDERS WILLIAM N. orphans--McEwins, Monroe County--No date given--1064--17--2Chers.

WILLIS JAMES--Edwards, Talbot County--S. Riley--20 May 1846--1065--17--2Cher.

MOORE ELIJAH SR.--116th. Hancock County--20 July 1834--1066--17--2Cher.

BATTS MCALLEN--Hampton, Newton County--24 January 1834--1067--17--2Cher.

WILLIAMSON WILLIAM--Petersons, Montgomery County--B.H. Moultrie--18 May 1846--1--17--2Cher.

McGUFFE JOHN JR.--Foots, DeKalb County--30 August 1834--1069--17--2Cher.

LINSEYS JAMES orphans--Pearces, Wilkinson County--7 December 1840--1082--17--2Cher.

WILSON JAMES--Espys, Clarke County--T.R. Bloom--9 February 1846--1083--17--2Cher.

PRATT DANIEL--Sullivans, Jones County--16 February 1835--1084--17--2Cher.

JARRARD JOSIAH D.--Brocks, Habersham County--12 March 1836--1094--17--2Cher.

YATES JOSEPH--Gouldings, Lowndes County--9 June 1843--1095--17--2Cher.

CLEMONS WILLIAM--732nd, Dooly County--10 November 1838--1096--17--2Cher.

BRADLEY PRESSLEY--Woods, Morgan County--25 November 1836--1097--17--2Cher.

SHACKELFORD JAMES L.--Edwards, Franklin County--4 December 1835--58--18--2Cher.

NEAL STEPHEN--Holleys, Franklin County--6 May 1836--59--18--2Cher.

MAXEY JEREMIAH--Heads, Butts County--29 January 1836--60--18--2Cher.

MITCHELL SAMUEL D.--Athens, Clark County--15 June 1835--172--18--2Cher.

HALL THOMAS L.--Marshes, Thomas County--C. Day--20 May 1846--173--18--2Cher.

HARVILL ELLIS--Whipples, Wilkinson County--16 September 1836--174--18--2Cher.

McBRIDE JAMES JR.--Gittens, Fayette County--18 February 1835--175--18--2Cher.

WATSON ELIJAH--Masons, Washington County--12 May 1834--283--18--2Cher.

CARRUTHERS JAMES--71st, Burke County--28 October 1834--284--18--2Cher.

REED JOHN B.--Alexanders, Jefferson County--28 October 1834--285--18--2Cher.

SHACKLEFORD PHILIP--Holidays, Jackson County--5 November 1835--286--18--2Cher.

THORNTON VINCENT R.--140th, Greene County--21 September 1835--398--18--2Cher.

GRESHAM JEREMIAH--Jones, Lincoln County--15 December 1834--399--18--2Cher.

CASH JOHN JR.--Mitchells, Jackson County--1 June 1840--400--18--2Cher.

PACE BASSEL--Dericks, Henry County--15 September 1839--401--18--2Cher.

POSEY MIRE orph.--Ellis, Pulaski County--C. Day--11 May 1846--402--18--2Cher.

JOHNSON SURWOOD B.--Howells, Troup County--22 March 1843--500--18--2Cher.

LIGHTFOOT THOMAS--Comers, Jones County--7 March 1835--501--18--2Cher.

HATCHER WILLIAM--1st Section, Cherokee County--C. Day--11 May 1846--502--18--2Cher.

MATTOX NATHAN--Smiths, Elbert County--22 March 1843--503--18--2Cher.

JENKINS REASON--Smiths, Houston County--7 March 1835--598--18--2Cher.

BARNES JOHN M.--Mortons, DeKalb County--7 April 1836--599--18--2Cher.

McGANGHEY JAMES--454th, Walton County--9 March 1836--600--18--2Cher.

MURRAY DAVID SCOTT--McDowells, Lincoln County--23 June 1835--18--2Cher.

MONCRIEF JAMES--McMillons, Lincoln County--22 April 1837--693--18--2Cher.

SHICK JOHN JR.--Sanderlins, Chatham County--30 April 1835--694--18--2Cher.

DEAN JAMES--Iversons, Houston County--8 January 1835--695--18--2Cher.

MORGAN JAMES--Shaddix, Coweta County--26 March 1836--782--18--2Cher.

FILGRIM MITCHELL SR.--Fields, Habersham County--20 June 1834--783--18--2Cher.

COGBURN JOHN A.--Vinnings, Putnam County--Harris & Millen--16 Feb 1846--784--18--2Cher.

PETERS JOHN--415th, Walton County--13 November 1834--785--18--2Cher.

PERDEE LARKIN--Salem, Baldwin County--11 December 1833--786--18--2Cher.

BUSBY ALLEN--Walkers, Houston County--E. Austin--20 May 1846--827--18--2Cher.

TATE JOHN--Hughes, Habersham County--5 January 1837--828--18--2Cher.

WATKINS JAMES W.--Halls, Butts County--13 November 1837--829--18--2Cher.

BATTEY JOSEPH S.--Graves, Putnam County--C. Day--11 May 1846--830--18--2Cher.

RIDDLE TAZY or.--Marshalls, Crawford Co.--Caleb P. Bowen--gr. as 131--831--18--2Cher.

RIDDLE ANN orphan--Marshalls, Crawford County--see Riddle Tazy--831--18--2Cher.

RIDDLE ELIZABETH orphan--Marshalls, Crawford County--see Riddle Tazy--831--18--2Cher.

FINCHER JOSHUA--Reids, Gwinnett County--4 August 1837--868--18--2Cher.

GIRKIE MARGARET--25th, Glynn County--6 December 1834--869--18--2Cher.

OTWELL GILFORD R.--Allens, Henry County--21 November 1836--870--18--2Cher.

DEMPHY LAWRENCE--Valleans, Chatham County--21 November 1838--871--18--2Cher.

MALONE SPENCER--McLins, Butts County--27 June 1843--904--18--2Cher.

SHIPP ABNER--417th, Walton County--J.S. Richardson--29 May 1847--905--18--2Cher.

PENDLEY HEZEKIAH--Barkers, Gwinnett County--J.S. Richardson--29 May 1847--906--18--2Cher.

WILSON ANDREW orph.--Gwinnett County--Caleb P. Brown--21 Sept. 1857--907--18--2Cher.

WILKES SOLOMON B.--640th, Dooly Co.--William C. Cash--19 January 1852--908--18--2Cher.

BEADWELL JAMES S.--271st, McIntosh County--29 March 1836--909--18--2Cher.

MINYARD FLEMING--Chandlers, Franklin County--1 July 1843--910--18--2Cher.

LOCKHART ELIEL--Graves, Lincoln County--16 May 1837--911--18--2Cher.

THOMPSON WILLIAM L.--Williams, Jasper County--24 February 1835--940--18--2Cher.

WILLIAMS JENKINS D.--Bruces, Greene County--23 December 18442?--941--18--2Cher.

DUKE GREEN R.--Mitchells, Jackson County--12 February 1835--942--18--2Cher.

LUCKETT THOMAS H.--Underwoods, Putnam County--1 July 1843--943--18--2Cher.

MASSEY SIMEON--Shows, Muscogee County--3 April 1843--944--18--2Cher.

HINKLE SOLOMON--Chastains, Habersham County--B.H. Moultrie--12 Feb. 1846--968--18--2Cher.

SHERROD JAMES--Woods, Jefferson County--H. Willingham--12 May 1846--969--18--2Cher.

SMITH ELIJAH--Hobbs, Laurens County--1 July 1848--970--18--2Cher.

CHAMBERLIN JAMES--494th, Upson County--No date given--971--18--2Cher.

LUCAS CHARLES--Hutsons, Newton County--No date given--972--18--2Cher.

MITCHUM HENDRICK--Stantons, Newton Co.--W.B. Johnson--gr. as 2D 3S--9 May 46--972--18--2Cher.

RICHARDSON JOHN--Norris, Monroe County--1 July 1843--974--18--2Cher.

DUNKIN PETER SR.--Shearers, Coweta Co.--B.C. Moultrie--12 February 1846--975--18--2Cher.

PERKINS JOHN--Jordans, Bibb County--1 July 1843--992--18--2Cher.

TURNER WILLIAM--Cleggs, Walton County--10 April 1843--993--18--2Cher.

ROWLS JESSE--Maddens, Pike County--W.P. Johnson--25 July 1848--994--18--2Cher.

SEALE WM. H.--Bensons, Lincoln County--1 July 1843--995--18--2Cher.

STANSELL JOHN W.--Clintons, Campbell Co.--W.W. Paine & J.R. Compton--9 Sept 53--996--18--2Cher.

TERRY JOHN--Leveretts, Lincoln Co.--(J.H. Coryell)--12 May 1846--997--18--2Cher.

TUCKER ANNA widow--Duprees, Washington Co.--(J.H. Coryett)--12 May 1846--998--18--2Cher.

PARSONS ROBERT--Woods, Jefferson County--16 December 1841--1009--18--2Cher.

HAISTEN HARRISON--Hitchcock, Muscogee Co.--B.H. Moultrie--12 Feby. 1846--1010--18--2Cher.

BUSH NATHAN--Jordans, Bibb County--4 August 1837--1011--18--2Cher.

DARDEN ABNER--601st, Taliaferro Co.--Harris & Millen--16 February 1846--1012--18--2Cher.

McEVER ANDREW--Cleghorns, Madison County--J.H. Caryell--12 May 1846--1013--18--2Cher.

McGEE LEVIN--Howells, Troup County--12 August 1844--1014--18-2Cher.

STARRITT JAMES--Dyers, Habersham County--J.H. Caryell--12 May 1846--1015--18--2Cher.

CLARK THOMAS J.--Cummings, Elbert County--25 September 1834--1016--18--2Cher.

MILLS HENRY--122nd, Richmond County--S.G. Gay--12 May 1846--1017--18--2Cher.

SCOTT JOHN--Sealleiys, Talbot Co.--Harris & Millen--16 February 1846--1018--18--2Cher.

HARRISON TILMAN--Liddles, Jackson County--16 May 1843--1019--18--2Cher.

McFEE HENDERSON--Dobbs, Hall County--1 July 1843--1020--18--2Cher.

TONEY HENCRICK--Mangums, Franklin County--1 July 1843--1021--18--2Cher.

HEAD JAMES B.--Loveless, Gwinnett County--1 July 1843--1022--18--2Cher.

SLAYTON JOHN--Griers, Meriwether County--J.H. Coryett--12 May 1846--1023--18--2Cher.

FLANIGAN KENIAN--Frasiers, Monroe County--No date given--1024--18--2Cher.

BEST JACOB B.--259th, Scriven County--10 February 1837--1--19--2Cher.

SAXON DAVIS--604th, Taliaferro County--13 February 1843--74--19--2Cher.

SHEFTALL EMANUEL--7th, Chatham County--14 June 1843--75--19--2Cher.

HAYNES JOHNSON--Whisenhunts, Carroll Co.--W.D. Conyers--12 February 1846--148--19--2Cher.

DUNN JAMES M.--Robinsons, Putnam County--W.D. Conyers--13 December 1845--149--19--2Cher.

COOK JOHN JR.--Atkinsons, Coweta County--6 June 1843--222--19--2Cher.

STONE JOHN W.--Williams, Jasper County--W.D. Conyers--13 Dec. 1845--223--19--2Cher.

JONES WILLIAM B.--Butts, Monroe County--16 January 1838--296--19--2Cher.

SLATER JAMES--Jordans, Bibb County--26 June 1841--297--19--2Cher.

EVERITT THOMAS--Pearces, Houston County--29 March 1836--370--
19--2Cher.

HILL ELIZABETH widow--Harris, Columbia County--1 July 1843--371--
19--2Cher.

HALL DEMPSEY--789th, Sumter County--W.D. Conyers--12 Feb. 1846--
444--19--2Cher.

CUMMING JOHN--Valleaus, Chatham County--10 March 1834--445--19--
2Cher.

BIRDSONG PARRIS M.--Scroggins, Oglethorpe County--10 February
1840--518--19--2Cher.

DOWNER JOSEPH--Howells, Elbert County--1 July 1843--519--19--
2Cher.

RANDLE JOHN S.--Robinsons, Putnam County--21 December 1839--592--
19--2Cher.

McCOY JAMES--Smiths, Campbell County--20 December 1836--593--19--
2Cher.

SAVAGE ZACHARIAH--119th, Richmond County--5 January 1835--666--
19--2Cher.

TERRY JOHN W.--Foots, DeKalb County--W.D. Conyers--12 Feb. 1846--
667--19--2Cher.

ANTHONY JOHN M.--Chambers, Gwinnett County--25 December 1838--
740--19--2Cher.

EDWARDS LITTLETON C.--417th, Walton County--1 July 1843--741--
19--2Cher.

MICKLER WILLIAM--Hobkerks, Camden County--B.H. Moultrie--12 Feb.
1846--814--19--2Cher.

ST JOHNS THOMAS--Martins, Newton County--5 September 1840--815--
19--2Cher.

DASHER CRISTIAN H.--9th, Effingham County--W.B. Johnson--12 Feb.
1846--888--19--2Cher.

HUBBARD JOHN S.--Guices, Oglethorpe County--2 December 1835--
889--19--2Cher.

JONES WILLIS B.--Clarks, Elbert County--22 December 1836--962--
19--2Cher.

WHITEHEAD WILLIAM SR.--Holidays, Jackson County--29 November
1838--963--19--2Cher.

GRAY JOHN M.--Parhams, Harris County--21 July 1835--1036--19--
2Cher.

JONES MOSES--Jenkins, Oglethorpe County--22 June 1843--1037--19--
2Cher.

CHALMERS JOHN M.--2nd Section, Cherokee County--18 November
1840--1110--19--2Cher.

McCULLOCH HARDY D.--516th, Dooly County--2 January 1840--1111--
19--2Cher.

WHALEY JAMES--Harralsons, Troup County--15 November 1838--1184--
19--2Cher.

RUMSAY RICHARD--Willis, Franklin County--5 March 1838--1185--19--
2Cher.

BOLER RODA widow--Graves, Lincoln County--11 December 1835--
1258--19--2Cher.

GLOZIER JOHN--Hamptons, Newton County--8 December 1841--1259--
19--2Cher.

SPENCE JOSEPH C.--Chambers, Gwinnett County--17 December 1840--
1332--19--2Cher.

HILLSMAN PASCAL W.--Coxes, Talbot County--1 July 1843--1--1--
3Cher.

PIERCE THOMAS--Cannons, Wilkinson County--19 February 1839--2--
1--3Cher.

RHODES WILLIAM--601st, Taliaferro County--20 June 1843--3--1--
2Cher.

PHELPS WILLIAM W.--Berrys, Butts County--S.C. Candler--7 May
1846--4--1--3Cher.

RICH GEORGE W.--Harrisons, Decatur County--S.C. Candler--13
February 1847--5--1--3Cher.

REEVES ABNER--166th, Wilkes County--26 March 1841--6--1--3Cher.

MAYNOR RECY H.--Manns, Crawford County--20 December 1842--7--1--
3Cher.

RUNNELLS GEORGE W.--Bishops, Henry County--16 October 1851--152--
1--3Cher.

FURGERSON BURREL--Stewarts, Troup County--21 December 1837--153--
1--3Cher.

SMITH ARCHIBALD his orphans--Petersons, Montgomery County--8 March
1844--154--1--3Cher.

TATE SAMUEL--Jones, Hall County--Joseph Brice--7 May 1846--155--
1--3Cher.

COVINGTON SALLY, widow--Daniels, Hall County--B.H. Moultrie--
18 May 1846--156--1--3Cher.

JAMES EBENEZER--Normans, Wilkes County--A. Goolsby--8 May 1846--
157--1--3Cher.

PECK MARY widow--148th, Greene County--No date given--158--1--
3Cher.

REGISTER SARAH widow--Cowarts, Lowndes County--No date given--
159--1--3Cher.

CHATFIELD ISAAC orphan--Allens, Bibb County--28 June 1844--160--
1--3Cher.

HARRELL RODHAM--555th, Upson County--B. Lewis--14 May 1846--161--
1--3Cher.

MAY JOSEPH--759th, Sumter County--22 December 1835--162--1--3Cher.

GAINER SAMUEL--458th, Early County--26 April 1837--163--1--3Cher.

ATKINSON LAZARUS SR.--Slaughters, Greene County--28 June 1843--
288--1--3Cher.

BRYAN GEORGE W.--Stanfields, Campbell County--R.R. Cuyler--12
May 1846--289--1--3Cher.

McCLUNG REUBEN--Loveless, Gwinnett County--1 October 1844--290--
1--3Cher.

LYONS JAMES H.--Washburns, Pulaski County--J. Allen--19 May 1844--291--1--3Cher.

MARCHMAN WILLIAM R.--Tompkins, Putnam County--No date given--292--1--3Cher.

RICHARD JOHN--Trouts, Hall County--No date given--293--1--3Cher.

TURNER ZADOCK--118th, Hancock County--P.M. Compston--12 May 1846--294--1--3Cher.

MORE ALFRED D.--Peacocks, Washington County--W.D. Conyers--12 Feb. 1846--295--1--3Cher.

OLIN STEPHEN--Athens, Clarke County--W.D. Conyers--12 February 1846--296--1--3Cher.

WILLSON JAMES--Belchers, Jasper County--W.D. Conyers--12 Feb. 1846--297--1--3Chers.

WOOD ROBERT--Heards, DeKalb County--R.R. Cuyler--12 May 1846--298--1--3Cher.

REYNOLDS SHARP his orphs.--McGills, Lincoln Co.--L.H. Buscre?--21 Nov 57--405--1--3Cher.

BROOKS ELIJAH--Hoods, Henry County--10 November 1842--406--1--3Cher.

DAVIS CHARLES--Robinsons, Fayette County--6 December 1839--407--1--3Cher.

RAWLS WILLIAM--Hutchinsons, Columbia County--11 August 1842--408--1--3Cher.

REID NATHANIEL--Rhodes, DeKalb County--17 November 1838--409--1--3Cher.

INGE CHARLES--604, Taliaferro County--No date given--410--1--3Cher.

SMITH ROBERT--Nelsums, Elbert County--1 May 1843--411--1--3Cher.

SANDERS JOHN--334th, Wayne County--S.C. Candler--28 April 1846--412--1--3Cher.

HIGGASON WILLIAM--Crows, Pike County--18 February 1836--413--1--3Cher.

HOWARD JAMES W.--672nd, Harris County--5 December 1834--506--1--3Cher.

FALKNER JAMES W.--Willinghams, Harris County--24 January 1839--507--1--3Cher.

HENLY WILLIAM--Maguires, Gwinnett County--13 December 1834--508--1--3Cher.

RENFRO ALFRED--Pearces, Houston County--11 August 1842--509--1--3Cher.

ROBINSON JESSE--334th, Wayne County--25 May 1836--510--1--3Cher.

KENNEDY JOHN C.--Peuriofys, Henry County--No date given--511--1--3Cher.

BUTTS WILLIAM N.--Maguires, Morgan County--2 February 1837--512--1--3Cher.

McDOWELL THOMAS C.--Kellums, Talbot County--1 February 1839--513--1--3Cher.

NAISWORTHY WILLIAM--73rd, Burke County--30 April 1836--514--1--3Cher.

MAYO HARMON--633rd, Dooly County--J.C. Coal--20 September 1845--594--1--3Cher.

WILLIAMS LEWIS--Stricklands, Meriwether County--16 June 1843--595--1--3Cher.

SMITH JOHN--Nisbets, Newton County--J.W. Davis--8 September 1845--596--1--3Cher.

CHILDS BENJAMIN--Sewells, Franklin County--B.H. Moultrie--19 May 1846--597--1--3Cher.

WILLIAMS JESSE--McDaniels, Pulaski County--12 February 1847--598--1--3Cher.

NUNNERY HENRY--Pounds, Twiggs County--30 April 1834--599--1--3Cher.

DANIEL WILLIAM B.--55th, Emanuel County--4 November 1835--600--1--3Cher.

EDENFIELD DAVID JR.--59th, Emanuel County--20 December 1838--601--1--3Cher.

WOOD JOHN--Mosleys, Coweta County--12 December 1837--667--1--3Cher.

LANDERS BENJAMIN--Fenns, Clarke County--25 June 1835--668--1--3Cher.

YOUNGBLOOD NATHAN--Salem, Baldwin County--9 January 1839--669--1--3Cher.

WATKINS WILLIAM--Vinings, Putnam County--J.B. Williams--19 March 1846--670--1--3Cher.

MORRIS ELIZABETH widow--Ellis, Pulaski Co.--J.B. Williams--4 April 1846--671--1--3Cher.

RAY DEMPSEY J.--Grays, Henry County--Jesse Roberts--17 November 1847--672--1--3Cher.

CAMP RUSSELL--249th, Walton County (J.B. Williams)--3 December 1847--673--1--3Cher.

SMITH ISAAC--Peacocks, Washington County--B.H. Moultie--Date not given--674--1--3Cher.

COOK JOSHUA--142nd, Green County--31 March 1837--675--1--3Cher.

BLALOCK REUBEN--588th, Upson County--S.C. Candler--13 April 1846--676--1--3Cher.

GRAY SAMPSON--Peurifoys, Henry County--29 October 1838--677--1--3Cher.

LESTER JACOB JR.--Hargroves, Oglethorpe County--1 July 1843--678--1--3Cher.

JUSTISS JOHN H.R.--Nights, Morgan County--1 July 1843--679--1--3Cher.

WRIGHT ELVIRA widow--Doziers, Columbia County--22 June 1843--680--1--3Cher.

TERRY JOHN--Givens, DeKalb County--16 November 1836--681--1--3Cher.

GRIFFIN S. BENNETT--Elsworth, Bibb County--30 November 1837--682--1--3Cher.

YOUNG LUCRETIA widow--Newmans, Thomas County--26 November 1840--716--1--3Cher.

SPOONER ADAM--Killens, Decatur County--29 November 1837--717--1--3Cher.

MONTGOMERY JOHN--Morgans, Madison County--22 December 1836--718--1--3Cher.

STROZIER PETER--166th, Wilkes County--8 November 1841--719--1--3Cher.

MOORE DANIEL--Shearers, Coweta County--28 August 1837--720--1--3Cher.

JONES WILEY--Colliers, Monroe County--1 July 1843--721--1--3Cher.

WHITLOW WILLIAM--Thomas, Clarke County--W. Eason--7 May 1846--722--1--3Cher.

CLARK JOHN M.--Bracketts, Newton County--J.A. Moore--19 May 1846--723--1--3Cher.

BEALLE JOHN W.--Culbreaths, Columbia Co.--Jno. Thompson Jr.--17 May 1846--724--1--3Cher.

TUCKER ELIZABETH widow--Salem, Baldwin County--No date given--725--1--3Cher.

EDMUNDSON JAMES--Nisbets, Newton County--17 June 1843--726--1--3Cher.

HOWARD JOHN H.--Perrys, Baldwin County--W.C. Austin--7 May 1846--727--1--3Cher.

MARTIN JAMES E.--Bakers, Liberty County--T.D. Johnson--10 December 1845--728--1--3Cher.

COPP BELTON A.--Hobkirks, Camden County--5 December 1835--729--1--3Cher.

MARCHMAN JOHN--Tompkins, Putnam County--W.W. McClung--7 February 1846--730--1--3Cher.

SMITH ROBERT N.--104th, Hancock County--27 November 1840--731--1--3Cher.

OVERTON JAMES--Bishops, Henry County--W.D. Conyers--13 December 1845--732--1--3Cher.

STUART ALEXANDER--4th Section, Cherokee County--(P.M. Compton)--12 May 1846--739--1--3Cher.

PALMER MARTIN--27th, Glynn County--2 December 1835--740--1--3Cher.

LOYD ISHAM--Taylors, Jones County--1 July 1843--741--1--3Cher.

BOSWORTH SARAH, widow--Fews, Muscogee County--P.M. Compton--12 May 1846--742--1--3Cher.

BIRD BELLINGS BRITT--Givens, DeKalb County--1 July 1843--743--1--3Cher.

JONES STEPHEN--Crawfords, Morgan County--No date given--744--1--3Cher.

JARNION EMERY--Nichols, Fayette Co.--P.M. Compton--17 February 1851--745--1--3Cher.

BROCK JOHN L.--Brocks, Habersham County--Wm. H. Davidson--5 June 1850--1185--20--3Cher.

FLOURNOY SIMON--Luncefords, Wilkes County--28 September 1838--1186--20--3Cher.

NIGHT JESSY--Bushes, Burke County--C. Day--9 May 1846--1187--20--3Cher.

FLEMING SAMUEL--Christees, Jefferson County--1 July 1843--1188--20--3Cher.

DELAIGH NICHOLAS--122nd, Richmond County--16 June 1843--1245--20--3Cher.

McDONALD HENRY--Heards, DeKalb County--Jas. Blackman--12 May 1846--1246--20--3Cher.

LON JESSE--454th, Walton County--Jas. Blackman--12 May 1846--1247--20--3Cher.

BECKHAM LABAN--Crows, Pike County--27 September 1844--1248--20--3Cher.

DICKINSON JAND orphans--Deavours, Habersham County--No date given--1249--20--3Cher.

WARD WILLIAM--R. Browns, Habersham County--J. Blackman--12 May 1846--1250--20--3Cher.

SOLOMONS GODWIN--Tryers, Telfair County--4 December 1837--1251--20--3Cher.

REAVES IRWIN--109th, Hancock County--J.R. Wood--7 May 1846--1252--20--3Cher.

GODDARD JOHN--Mullins, Carroll County--G. Kingsbury--7 May 1846--20--3Cher.

DRAKE WILLIAM--Maddens, Pike County--27 September 1844--1254--20--3Cher.

ANDREWS JOSEPH--26th, Glynn County--O.F. Adams--31 January 1854--1255--20--3Cher.

CASON JOSEPH--Lamberths, Fayette County--1 July 1843--1256--20--3Cher.

SMITH JAMES--454th, Walton Co.--W.W. Paine & J.R. Compton--9 Sept. 1853--1257--20--3Cher.

NEW ELIJAH--Bracketts, Newton Co.--W.W. Paine & J.R. Compton--9 Sept. 1853--1258--20--3Cher.

BURNETT ISAAC SR.--Kendricks, Monroe County--4 November 1840--1259--20--3Cher.

HAMMOCK ASA A.--Brewers, Walton County--5 June 1843--1260--20--3Cher.

BEALL ALPHEUS--Pates, Wilkinson County--14 July 1831--1261--20--3Cher.

TUCKER JOEL T.--Mayos, Wilkinson County--1 July 1833--1262--20--3Cher.

WALLER BENJAMIN--108th, Hancock County--20 June 1843--1286--20--3Cher.

MITCHAM JOHN--Griffins, Meriwether County--W.H. Davidson--5 June 1850--1287--20--3Cher.

RODERICK JOSEPH--516th, Dooly County--12 July 1838--1288--20--3Cher.

HAMMOCK JEREMIAH--177th, Wilkes County--10 November 1834--1289--20--3Cher.

BLAKEY COUNCIL--105th, Baldwin County--W.H. Davidson--5 June 1850--1290--20--3Cher.

DOUGLASS ROBERT M.--Harris, Crawford County--1 July 1843--1291--20--3Cher.
PEPPER KELLEY--Givens, DeKalb County--24 June 1843--1292--20--3Cher.
SLATON WILLIAM--Pollards, Wilkes County--B.H. Moultrie--19 May 1846--1--1--4Cher.
LANE RICHARD--Peavys, Bulloch County--Spencer Riley--8 September 1853--82--1--4Cher.
HOPPER SARAH, widow--Seay, Hall County--Paine & Compton--9 Sept. 1853--83--1--4Cher.
REDD WILLIAM A.--Talleys, Troup County--Paine & Compton--9 Sept. 1853--164--1--4Cher.
ANDERSON STERLING (his orphans)--Raineys, Twiggs Co.--No date of Grant--165--1--4Cher.
KELLY TERRELL--Newsoms, Warren County--No date of Grant--246--1--4Cher.
DEAN GEORGE--Cokers, Troup Co.--W.W. Paine & J.R. Compton--9 Sept. 1853--247--1--4Cher.
KENDRICK JAMES R.--174th, Wilkes County--15 May 1839--326--1--4Cher.
WAMBLE ALLEN B. (orph)--Haygoods, Washington County--26 December 1842--327--1--4Cher.
PRUETT THOMAS--Barkers, Gwinnett County--9 June 1843--406--1--4Cher.
RIGIL WYTHEL--Raineys, Twiggs County--18 December 1837--407--1--4Cher.
WRIGHT DAVID--Hanners, Campbell County--No date given--486--1--4Cher.
CAWTHEN JAMES--Baileys, Butts County--28 November 1839--487--1--4Cher.
IVEY CHARLES--174th, Wilkes County--7 September 1837--564--1--4Cher.
WALDROUP MATHEW--Allens, Henry Co.--W.W. Paine & J.R. Compton--9 Sept. 1853--565--1--4Cher.
BRIDGES BENNETT--Sanders, Jones Co.--W.W. Paine & J.R. Compton--9 Sept. 1853--642--1--4Cher.
THIGPEN MALANTON--395th, Emanuel County--No date given--643--1--4Cher.
NORMAN BENJAMIN--Hintons, Wilkes County--28 February 1838--719--1--4Cher.
THOMASON THOMAS L.--Nesbets, Newton County--15 May 1837--720--1--4Cher.
WHITE DAVID T.--Robinsons, Putnam County--Spencer Riley--8 September 1853--795--1--4Cher.
SANFORD JEREMIAH--104th, Hancock County--Spencer Riley--8 Sept. 1853--796--1--4Cher.
McMICHAEL GRIFFIN--Halls, Butts County--Spencer Riley--8 Sept. 1853--797--1--4Cher.

GREEN ALEXANDER S.--604th, Taliaferro County--1 October 1836--798--1--4Cher.

KNOLES WASHINGTON--Georges, Appling Co.--Spencer Riley--8 Sept. 1853--860--1--4Cher.

KNOLES WASHINGTON--Georges, Appling County--3-22-1843 (Granted twice)--860--1--4Cher.

PATE STEPHEN M.--Duprees, Morgan County--1 July 1843--861--1--4Cher.

STEPHENS JAMES--Candlers, Bibb Co.--W.W. Paine & J.R. Compton--9 Sept. 1853--862--1--4Cher.

CHESSER MATHEW--Brewtons, Tattnall County--14 December 1835--863--1--4Cher.

HUGUENIN EDWARD H.--Houstons, Chatham County--1 July 1843--864--1--4Cher.

ORSBURN DAVID--Darings, Butts County--27 November 1839--865--1--4Cher.

McKNIGHT SAMUEL--Brewers, Monroe Co.--W.W. Paine & J.R. Compton--9 Sept. 1853--866--1--4Cher.

WALKER JESSE SR.--756th, Sumter County--No date given--867--1--4Cher.

TURNER ANDREW (his orphans)--Burnetts, Lowndes County--5 November 1835--868--1--4Cher.

RICHARDS WILLIAM M.--Clarks, Morgan County--No date given--869--1--4Cher.

DANIEL REUBEN F.--2nd Section, Cherokee County--18 November 1840--870--1--4Cher.

TRACY ELEAZER (his orphans)--Harris, Columbia County--21 December 1842--871--1--4Cher.

COOTS JOHN--Kellums, Talbot Co.--W.W. Paine & J.R. Compton--9 Sept. 1853--910--1--4Cher.

CADE DRURY B.--192nd, Elbert County--23 June 1843--873--1--4Cher.

ELLIOTT MARTHA widow--Dawsons, Jasper Co.--J.R. Compton--3 Nov. 1853--874--1--4Cher.

FOARD JAMES A.--Morris, Crawford Co.--W.W. Paine & J.R. Compton--9 Sept. 1853--910--1--4Cher.

CONE STEPHEN--Swaines, Thomas Co.--W.W. Paine & J.R. Compton--9 Sept. 1853--911--1--4Cher.

OGLESBY JAMES A.--McClains, Newton County--2 November 1837--912--1--4Cher.

EDWARDS BERRY--Edwards, Talbot Co.--W.W. Paine & J.R. Compton--9 Sept. 1853--913--1--4Cher.

WRIGHT MICHAEL--Liddells, Jackson County--A.J. Goggins--3 March 1846--914--1--4Cher.

TANNER JOHN--Bracketts, Newton County--No date given--915--1--4Cher.

PEEL JAMES--Hitchcocks, Muscogee County--No date given--916--1--4Cher.

HUDGINS JOSIAH--Balls, Monroe County--1 July 1843--917--1--4Cher.

PARRAMORE SARAH widow--Smiths, Houston County--18 May 1843--918--
1--4Cher.
REEVES THOMAS--Adams, Columbia County--W.G. Walker--3 April 1846
--919--1--4Cher.
JOHNSON MARTIN--Goodwins, Houston County--1 July 1843--935--1--
4Cher.
STEPHENS JOHN--Currys, Wilkinson County--24 December 1840--936--
1--4Cher.
BURNAM WILLIAM JR.--Folsoms, Lowndes County--Spencer Riley--8
Sept. 1853--937--1--4Cher.
BOGGASS JEREMIAH--Coxes, Morgan County--Spencer Riley--8 Sept..
1853--938--1--4Cher.
DASHER THOMAS--Jones, Bulloch County--7 December 1836--939--1--
4Cher.
McARTHUR DANIEL--Wootens, Telfair County--No date given--940--
1--4Cher.
POWELL WILLIAM JR.--Gittens, Fayette Co.--W.W. Paine & J.R.
Compton--9 Sept. 1853--941--1--4Cher.
BRYAN JOHN H.--430rd, Early County--W.W. Paine & J.R. Compton--
9 Sept. 1853--942--1--4Cher.
COCKRAN CHEADLE--Stanfields, Campbell County--27 September 1844--
943--1--4Cher.
COLQUIT BENJAMIN--Whitakers, Crawford Co.--W.W. Paine & J.R.
Compton--9 Sept. 53--944--1--4Cher.
DURDEN LEWIS--Everetts, Washington County--No date given--946--
1--4Cher.
WELLS HOWELL--Watsons, Marion County--No date given--947--1--
4Cher.
DAVIS JESSE H.--Bishops, Henry County--25 August 1836--313--2--
4--4Cher.
JOINER PETER--Baileys, Laurens County--27 August 1838--36--3--
4Cher.
LORD WHEATEN--Sinquefields, Washington County--23 January 1841--
37--3--4Cher.
SHEFFIELD WILLIAM SR.--104th, Hancock County--1 July 1843--108--
3--4Cher.
LUINGSTON MARTIN--McDaniels, Pulaski County--C. Day--21 May 1846
--109--3--4Cher.
HARRIS CHURCHWELL (his orphans)--Hangoods, Washington Co.--C.C.
Harrison--5 Dec. 57--180--3--4Cher.
WALKER JUDITH widow--Martins, Pike County--20 June 1835--181--
3--4Cher.
WILLIS JOSHUA--Cokers, Troup County--2 April 1835--252--3--4Cher.
HARRIS WESLEY--470th, Upson County--23 February 1838--253--3--
4Cher.
BLEDSOE BENJAMIN--Stanfiuelds, Campbell County--9 March 1836--
324--3--4Cher.
WHITE JAMES O.--Williams, Ware County--17 December 1834--325--
3--4Cher.

TURNER SHADRACK--McKrokles, Jasper County--6 December 1834--396--3--4Cher.

JOHNSON PHILIP--Seays, Hall County--17 May 1838--397--3--4Cher.

ARMSTRONG MARTIN--Iversons, Houston County--W.B. Brown--4 November 1845--468--3--4Cher.

ADAMS DAVID SR.--364th, Jasper County--28 November 1836--469--3--4Cher.

MURPHEY JEREMIAH--Clinton's, Campbell County--30 June 1843--540--3--4Cher.

CARSTARPHEN THOMAS C.--Manns, Crawford County--1 June 1843--541--3--4Cher.

ROGUEMORE THOMAS J.--Newbys, Jones County--B. Tison--19 May 1846--612--3--4Cher.

YOUNG MADISON--Wallis, Irwin County--W. Simmons--19 May 1846--613--3--4Cher.

MILLICAN CHARLES W.--Johnsons, DeKalb County--15 June 1842--757--3--4Cher.

DANELY SARAH widow--Elsworths, Bibb County--W.B. Johnston--25 July 1848--684--3--4Cher.

BAILS EMMOR--320th, Baldwin County--1 July 1843--756--3--4Cher.

COODY WILLIAM G.--Johnsons, DeKalb County--15 June 1843--757--3--4Cher.

SWAN WILLIAM--Gunns, Jefferson County--26 June 1843--828--3--4Cher.

ANDERSON JOHN--Johnsons, Warren Co.--Wm. B. Johnston--17 July 1848--829--3--4Cher.

EMERUS ELIZABETH widow--Valleaus, Chatham County--25 December 1837--900-3--4Cher.

SMITH PARKER W.--Smiths, Henry County--Wm. B. Johnston--25 July 1845--901--3--4Cher.

WILLIAMS WILSON orphan--Marshalls, Putnam Co.--A.S. Buarron--6 Nov. 1857--972--3--4Cher.

WINDHAM WILLIAM--Barrons, Houston Co.--W.B. Johnston--12 Feb. 1846--973--3--4Cher.

TROUP JAMES--271st, McIntosh County--1 July 1843--1044--3--4Cher.

McKINNON WILLIAM orphan--Cooks, Telfair County--A.C. Terhune--14 Dec. 1857--1045--3--4Cher.

MAXEY BENNETT H.--Halls, Oglethorpe County--Wm. S. Simmons--10 Apr. 1846--1116--3--4Cher.

GORDEN JOHN--Kellys, Elbert County--14 December 1842--1117--3--4Cher.

MATHEWS MORRIS--Bryans, Pulaski County--9 May 1839--1188--3--4Cher.

MAJORS ELEANOR widow--Bosticks, Twiggs County--W.B. Johnston--25 July 1848--1189--3--4Cher.

BONNER JOSIAH M.--656th, Troup County--John Foster--21 Oct. 1847--1260--3--4Cher.

McMULLAN DANIEL--318th, Baldwin County--29 April 1843--1261--3--4Cher.

ETHRIDGE JOSEPH S.--Mayos, Wilkinson County--H.A. Gibson--14 May 1846--181--17--4Cher.

HARWELL JOHN--Hughes, Habersham County--1 July 1843--182--17--4Cher.

ALLEN JOHN W.--Bosticks, Twiggs County--C. Campbell--7 May 184?--183--17--4Cher.

MORGAN DAVID B.--Varners, Meriwether County--E. Berry--8 November 1845--184--17--4Cher.

MERRIT FREDERICK JR.--Dixons, Irwin County--22 June 1843--185--17--4Cher.

LINDSEY THOMAS his orphans--Boyntons, Twiggs County--10 March 1854--242--17--4Cher.

BROWN EDWARD--Cannings, Elbert County--5 November 1834--243--17--4Cher.

BURNETT JOSEPH--Yorks, Stewart County--W.J. Wright--19 May 1846--244--17--4Cher.

GODFREY FREEMAN--Tuggles, Meriwether County--24 June 1837--245--17--4Cher.

THOMASON THOMAS G.--Smiths, Campbell County--1 July 1843--246--17--4Cher.

MAULDIN RICHARD--Barnetts, Lowndes Co.--Chisholm & Walthall--10 Nov. 1849--247--17--4Cher.

MYERS S.--Skidway Island, Chatham County--21 October 1834--248--17--4Cher.

MORGAN WILLIAM--Jones, Madison County--L.F. Harris--20 May 1846--249--17--4Cher.

ASKEW PERRY--Whisenhunts, Carroll County--23 December 1837--250--17--4Cher.

CROSS JAMES JR.--73rd, Burke County--L.F. Harris--20 May 1846--251--17--4Cher.

MYHAND THOMAS--Duprees, Morgan County--19 November 1839--252--17--4Cher.

CLIETT BAILEY C.--Griffins, Fayette Co.--P.M. Compton--17 Feb. 1851 (2nd Grant)--286--17--4Cher.

OWEN DANIEL--Coxes, Talbot County--13 May 1837--287--17--4Cher.

CLIETT BAILEY C.--Griffins, Fayette Co.--Chisholm & Walthall--10 Nov. 1849--286--17--4Cher.

HAWKINS NICHOLAS--304th, Putnam County--3 May 1843--288--17--4Cher.

WARREN JOHN--Whisenhunts, Carroll County--23 December 1837--289--17--4Cher.

LOVE ROBERT J.--Thomas, Clarke County--Ed Berry--6 April 1846--290--17--4Cher.

TURMAN JOEL C.--124th, Richmond Co.--Joel C. Turman--21 Jan. '53 (2nd Grant)--291--17--4Cher.

TURMAN JOEL C.--124th, Richmond Co.--Chisholm & Walthall--10 Nov. '49 (1st Grant)--291--17--4Cher.

HUGHES WILLIAM L.--Allens, Bibb Co.--P.M. Compton--17 February 1851--292--17--4Cher.

EVERETT SOLOMON--Wynns, Gwinnett County--P.M. Compton--17 February 1851--293--17--4Cher.

CARUTHERS JANE L. widow--Valleans, Chatham Co.--Edward F. Kinckley--10 May '49--294--17--4Cher.

NIX JOSEPH--Brocks, Habersham County--Edward F. Kinchley--10 May 1849--295--17--4Cher.

KITLEY JESSE--779th, Heard County--18 December 1834--309--17--4Cher.

PARK AUGUSTUS M.--Hemphills, Morgan Co.--P.M. Compton--17 February 1851--310--17--4Cher.

PRICE WILLIAM D.--Dyers, Habersham County--P.M. Compton--17 Feb. 1851--311-17--4Cher.

BARNETT WILLIAM--Hardemans, Oglethorpe County--27 November 1838--312--17--4Cher.

TOLLS WILLIAM--Newbys, Jones County--No date given--313--17--4Cher.

GILBERT THOMAS W.--Liddles, Jackson County--No date given--314--17--4Cher.

SAXON MARY--Harrisalds, Troup County--23 December 1836--315--17--4Cher.

TREWITT IRA--Sinclairs, Houston County--12 December 1835--316--17--4Cher.

WOODROFF WILLIAM B.--406th, Gwinnett County--P.M. Compton--17 Feb. 1851--317--17--4Cher.

CALLIER JOSEPH A.--Huchinsons, Columbia County--21 December 1837--397--16--4Cher.

CONNELLY WILLIAM--Seays, Hall County--S.W. Lee--17 February 1846--398--16--4Cher.

SNIDER ANTHONY--Clelands, Chatham County--9 May 1838--461--16--4Cher.

TIDWELL WILLIAM--Calhouns, Harris County--14 December 1836--462--16--4Cher.

KILLGORE ROWLAND--Blackstocks, Hall Co.--Raiford Ellis--30 Sept. 1845--463--16--4Cher.

METTS WRIGHT--Martins, Washington County--7 March 1837--464--16--4Cher.

CULBRETH THOMAS (Kiokee Creek)--Pecks, Columbia Co.--T.R. Bloom--11 May 1846--465--16--4Cher.

STRENGTH JAMES M.--373rd, Jasper County--No date given--466--16--4Cher.

AKENS SAMUEL--Marshs, Thomas County--Wm. B. Johnston--17 July 1848--467--16--4Cher.

GRAHAM ALLEX--Ricks, Laurens County--Wm. B. Johnston--17 July 1848--468--16--4Cher.

DELCESSILIM WM. E.--Halls, Camden County--Harris & Millen--30 October 1845--469--16--4Cher.

COOPER DAVID--Underwood, Putnam County--12 January 1834--470--16--4Cher.

MARTIN WILLIAM--Sumerlins, Bulloch County--19 December 1836--511--16--4Cher.

HARRIS WILLIAM--Wilsons, Pike County--21 December 1833--512--16--4Cher.

HODNETT BENJAMIN (Head of family)--Lovens, Henry Co.--W.B. Johnston--9 May '46--513--16--4Cher.

ASBELL JOSEPH--Fryers, Telfair County--4 May 1837--514--16--4Cher.

WALKER GEORGE W.--Williams, Walton County--T.R. Bloom--11 May 1846--515--16--4Cher.

BROWN SAMUEL B.--Colleys, Madison County--3 November 1840--516--16--4Cher.

THOMAS STEPHENS SR.--Athens, Clarke County--8 June 1843--517--16--4Cher.

SLATEN SEABORN--Dobbs, Hall County--W.B. Johnston--8 May 1846--518--16--4Cher.

NORRIS DANIEL N.--Ellsworth, Bibb County--C.M. Hitchcock--22 April 1846--538--16--4Cher.

GARRETT JOSEPH--114th, Hancock County--W.H. Fury--19 May 1846--539--16--4Cher.

TAYLOR THOMAS--Bosticks, Twiggs County--W.B. Johnston--9 May 1846--540--16--4Cher.

SWILL SARAH widow--Bakers, Liberty County--11 September 1837--541--16--4Cher.

HOOTEN JAMES--373rd, Jasper County--No date given--542--16--4Cher.

DICKSON CHARLES A.--735th, Troup County--23 June 1843--543--16--4Cher.

CRAMER JOSEPH--Howards, Oglethorpe County--10 December 1836--544--16--4Cher.

LILLY DAVID--103rd, Hancock County--Wm. B. Johnston--17 July 1848--545--16--4Cher.

KING HEROM--Hoods, Henry County--August 1837--546--16--4Cher.

REVIERE HARBERT B.--174th, Wilkes County--22 December 1837--549--16--4Cher.

SHEPHERD NATHAN--Herndons, Hall County--1 July 1843--550--16--4Cher.

PHILLIPS EPHRAIM SR.--395th, Emanuel County--No date given--551--16--4Cher.

HUGHES LITTLEBERRY--Youngs, Jefferson County--4 May 1843--553--16--4Cher.

WELLBORN JOHN R. (orphans)--Underwoods, Putnam County--No date given--554--16--4Cher.

NUTT DAVID M.--Halls, Butts County--No date given--555--16--4Cher.

JOHNSON JAMES--Camps, Baker County--Henry Mock--6 May 1846--37--16--1Cher.

HARDIN BENJAMIN B.--Doziers, Columbia County--21 June 1843--106--16--1Cher.

WOLF COUNCIL B.--Wrights, Laurens County--L.W. Cooper--21 Nov. 1853--139--16--1Cher.

JONES WILLIAM (Soldier)--103, Hancock County--No date given--140--16--1Cher.

MILLER LUCINDA (one of four orphans)--458, Early County--6 Feb. 1854--141--16--1Cher.

MILLER THOMAS (one of four orphans)--458, Early County--6 Feb. 1854--141--16--1Cher.

MILLER FRANCES (one of four orphans)--458, Early County--6 Feb. 1854--141--16--1Cher.

MILLER HENRY (one of four orphans)--458, Early County--6 Feb. 1854--141--16--1Cher.

TAYLOR NANCY widow--Bushes, Pulaski County--J.R. Compton--5 April 1854--169--16--1Cher.

AARON WILLIAM RILEY--Wares, Coweta County--No date given--170--16--1Cher.

NARON WILLIAM RILEY--Wares, Coweta County--No date given--170--16--1Cher.

MURPHEY WILLIAM--Lightfoots, Washington County--25 January 1838--196--16--1Cher.

STAFFORD ANDERSON--588th, Upson County--10 February 1838--218--16--1Cher.

HOLLAND TOBIAS--608th, Taliaferro County--22 July 1844--238--16--1Cher.

ELLIS JAMES JR.--Dawsons, Jasper County--No date given--239--16--1Cher.

BRADEN ELIAS--Herndons, Hall County--D.M. Jackson--19 March 1853 (66 Acres)--208--18--1Cher.

HUDGINS JOHN--Dyers, Habersham County--1.7 Acres--209--18--1Cher.

THOMPSON JOHN--Tuggles, Meriwether County--No date given--).75 Acres--210--18--1Cher.

BAGGETT JOHN--756th, Sumter Co.--J.R. Compton--3 Nov. 1853--73 Acres--244--18--1Cher.

WILKISON WILLIAM A.--Footes, DeKalb County--No date given (3 Acres)--245--18--1Cher.

FARMER ISHAM--Allisons, Pike County--W.W. Paine--3 Nov. 1853--(50.5 Acres)--275--18--1Cher.

BEARD JAMES A. SR.--Hughes, Habersham County--28 June 1843 (84 Acres)--304--18--1Cher.

PALMER WILSON--Mizells, Talbot County--W.W. Paine--3 Nov. 1853--(30 Acres)--71--19--1Cher.

HOUSE ELIAS--Hoods, Henry County--2 September 1843 (24 Acres)--73--19--1Cher.

HARFORD WILLIAM H.--15th, Liberty Co.--J.S. Richardson--17 April 1847 (45 Acres)--101--19--1Cher.

HOLTON ELIZABETH widow--Haygoods, Washington Co.--No date given-- (4 Acres)--102--19--1Cher.

HOOD ICHABOD--295th, Jasper County--15 March 1838 (74 Acres)-- 103--19--1Cher.

COLLINS JOHN--589th, Upson County--16 February 1837 (62 Acres)-- 115--19--1Cher.

MEDLIN RILEY soldier--Towers, Gwinnett County--2 Dec. 1841 (48 Acres)--116--19--1Cher.

ADAMS HEZEKIAH--Deans, DeKalb County--No date given (14 Acres)-- 117--19--1Cher.

BOGGS ARCHIBALD--398th, Richmond County--7 June 1843 (34 Acres)-- 118--19--1Cher.

DAWELY JAMES orphan--Jordans, Bibb County--No date given (12 Acres)--122--19--1Cher.

MARKS JANE L. widow--Flynns, Muscogee County--No date given-- (2 Acres)--123--19--1Cher.

CROSSLEY EDWARD--144th, Greene County--J.R. Compton--5 Apr. 1854 (24 Acres)--124--19--1Cher.

BADOLET MARY widow--Fitzpatricks, Chatham Co.--No date given-- (5 Acres)--125--19--1Cher.

MOON WILLIAM--Stewarts, Troup County--20 December 1839--19--4-- 2Cher.

TOWNSEND JAMES--Harps, Stewart County--D. Allen--17 February 1846--20--4--2Cher.

BARBER McGILBREY--Dilmans, Pulaski County--J.M. Cobb--15 April 1846--57--4--2Cher.

COLEY JOHN--Burnetts, Habersham County--T.R. Hason--19 November 1846--58--4--2Cher.

LANGLEY JOSIAH--Bryans, Monroe County--T.R. Hason--19 November 1846--95--4--2Cher.

MOSE DAVID--734th, Lee County--Saml. Con--8 September 1845--96-- 4--2Cher.

GORDAY ELIJAH--49th, Emanuel County--27 December 1833--133--4-- 2Cher.

SMITH HOWARD soldier--Harris, DeKalb County--13 May 1837--134-- 4--2Cher.

LILES WILLIAM--Lamberths, Fayette County--28 June 1838--171-- 4--2Cher.

BOTTOMS BURRELL--Allisons, Pike County--5 December 1837--172-- 4--2Cher.

SMITH IRA E.--Wares, Coweta County--15 December 1838--209--4-- 2Cher.

NOCKS JAMES (his orphans)--Sanderlins, Chatham County--1 July 1843--210--4--2Cher.

KNOX(?) JAMES (his orphans)--Sanderlins, Chatham County--1 July 1843--210--4--2Cher.

CLEMANS MARY M. widow--Prescotts, Twiggs Co.--W.P. Nichols--
8 Sept. 1845--247--4--2Cher.

SLAUGHTER JAMES--Davis, Jones County--11 May 1843--248--4--2Cher.

WALDER SAMUEL--Swinneys, Laurens County--W.P. Nichols--23 Oct.
1845--285--4--2Cher.

ELLIOTT LARKIN M. (his orphans)--Brocks, Habersham County--1 July
1843--286--4--2Cher.

JONES ANTHONY--Lynns, Warren County--16 November 1837--323--4--
2Cher.

THOMAS WILIE A.--Jordans, Bibb County--16 November 1837--324--
4--2Cher.

SMITH PATIN P. (Rev.)--Dyers, Habersham County--9 June 1843--
325--4--2Cher.

FIELDS DELILAH widow--Lamps, Jefferson County--1 July 1843--326--
4--2Cher.

CHANDLER ROBERT (soldier)--Wynns, Gwinnett County--7 December
1841--327--4--2Cher.

LEE VINCENT L.--24th, McIntosh County--5 December 1838--328--4--
2Cher.

WALKER JOHN--Mizells, Talbot County--4 October 1838--329--4--
2Cher.

REYNOLDS THOMAS (his orphans)--Parks, Walton County--7 July
1840--330--4--2Cher.

RENO JOHN JR.--Mercks, Hall County--Fletcher Freeman--8 May 1846
--331--4--2Cher.

VINCENT JESSE--Martins, Hall County--21 November 1836--332--4--
2Cher.

HOOPER JOHNSON M.--Adderholds, Campbell County--20 June 1843--
333--4--2Cher.

BEASLEY CYNTHIA widow--Gillis, DeKalb County--26 June 1843--
334--4--2Cher.

GIDDERY FREDERICK M.--Mattox, Lowndes County--23 March 1837--
335--4--2Cher.

BLALOCK JOHN H. orphan--398th. Richmond County--12 March 1847--
336--4--2Cher.

FULTON SAMUEL--295th. Jasper County--26 April 1843--337--4--
2Cher.

INGRAM WILLIAM F.--Gurns, Jones County--16 December 1842--338--
4--2Cher.

HARRIS ALBERT B.--McMillons, Lincoln County--26 August 1836--
339--4--2Cher.

LUKE ABRAHAM--Hills, Monroe Co. "See Ex Order 17 Nov 1845"--
22 Nov. 1837--340--4--2Cher.

WILLIAMS WILLIAM JR.--Coffees, Rabun County--Joseph Bangs--9 May
1846--341--4--2Cher.

HAVENER WILLIAM--120th. Richmond County--11 December 1839--342--
4--2Cher.

WATSON JOHN M. soldier--Hanners, Campbell Co.--5 May 1836--
(69.25 Acres)--307--13--2Cher.

INGRAM JOHN orphs. Ex Ord 19 Oct 1846--633, Dooly Co.--(87.75
Acres)--308--13--2Cher.

WATTS RILANT--56th, Emanuel County--18 July 1834--89 Acres--309--
13--2Cher.

HOPKINS BEDFORD--Robinsons, Harris Co.--J.N. Bethune--4 Nov.
1845--90.25 Acres--310--13--2Cher.

WOOTEN SIMON--Bryans, Pulaski County--Stewart Clayton--8 Sept.
1845--91.25 Acres--311--13--2Cher.

SHARP LEWIS J.--Ridens, Jackson County--31 May 1837--92.5 Acres
--312--13--2Cher.

MAURY HENRY--Brewers, Monroe County--6 September 1837--93.75
Acres--313--13--2Cher.

LAWSON DUDLEY--Durhams, Talbot County--T.B. Kees--10 Sept. 1845--
95 Acres--314--13--2Cher.

CREEMRNY REBECCA (Wrs)--Hands, Appling County--1 July 1843--
96.25 Acres--315--13--2Cher.

DARSEY REZIN--Harris, Columbia County--2 May 1835--97.5 Acres--
316--13--2Cher.

LYNCH CHRISTOPHER--Candlers, Bibb County--10 November 1838--
98.75 Acres--317--13--2Cher.

MORRIS JAMES--Edwards, Talbot County--9 February 1836--72 Acres--
19--20--2Cher.

HERRINGTON HENRY--Copelins, Houston County--5 April 1836--72
Acres--20--20--2Cher.

BROWNING MARGARET (WRS)--Morgans, Clarke Co.--1 July 1843--72
Acres--57--20--2Cher.

CRAIG ELBERT E.--Clelands, Chatham County--3 April 1835--72
Acres--58--20--2Cher.

GARDNER STARLING--Stewart, Warren Co.--W.B. Parker--10 Sept.
1845--72 Acres--95--20--2Cher.

BEARD WILLIAM M.--Athens, Clarke County--23 January 1839--72
Acres--96--20--2Cher.

HODGES AUGUSTUS G.W.--Salem, Baldwin County--23 November 1841--
72 Acres--133--20--2Cher.

VAUGHAN HENRY--Colliers, Monroe County--31 December 1835--72
Acres--134--20--2Cher.

STUBBLEFIELD CATHERINE widow--Norris, Monroe Co.--11 Jan. 1836--
72 Acres--171--20--2Cher.

BROOKS JOHN--Adams, Columbia County--17 November 1842--72 Acres--
172--20--2Cher.

BAYLES SARAH (WRS)--Downs, Warren County--23 February 1838--
72 Acres--209--20--2Cher.

McGEE PATRICK--Sanderlins, Chatham Co.--W.B. Parker--10 Sept.
1845--72 Acres--210--20--2Cher.

MARTIN JOHN--494th, Upson County--21 November 1836--72 Acres--
247--20--2Cher.

BAILEY HEZEKIAH--600th, Richmond County--1 July 1843--72 Acres--248--20--2Cher.

DINDY YOUNGSETT--Lawrences, Pike County--10 August 1836--72 Acres--285--20--2Cher.

HARGRAVE BRIGHT H.--Mullins, Carroll County--8 February 1836--72 Acres--286--20--2Cher.

WALKER LEVIN--Atkinsons, Coweta County--7 May 1839--72 Acres--323--20--2Cher.

HENDRICKS GILLFORD E.--Wilsons, Madison County--11 Dec. 1835--72 Acres--324--20--2Cher.

CHEEK WILLIAM B.--Crawfords, Franklin County--7 November 1838--40 Acres--16--6--3Cher.

SORELS JOHN--Walkers, Houston County--30 June 1843--43.5 Acres--17--6--3Cher.

BOWDOIN JOSIAH--365th, Jasper County--Mary Stephens--11 May 1846--45.25 Acres--48--6--3Cher.

WINGATE AMOS soldier--Delmans, Pulaski County--22 June 1843--47 Acres--49--6--3Cher.

SAMPSON ELIZABETH E.M.(WS)--123rd, Richmond County--29 June 1840--48.75 Acres--80--6--3Cher.

McCARTY GEORGE W.B. orphans--123rd, Richmond Co.--29 June 1840--48.75 Acres--80--6--3Cher.

BISSELL LEONARD--419th, Walton County--1 July 1843--50.5 Acres--81--6--3Cher.

GRANBERRY SAM M.--Sam Streetmans, Twiggs--J.M. Cantrell--11 May 1846--52.25 Acres--112--6--3Cher.

KERBY JAMES--Slaters, Bulloch County--1 July 1843--54 Acres--113--6--3Cher.

ROCHE JOHN--Fitzpatricks, Chatham County--16 December 1835--55.75 Acres--144--6--3Cher.

JOHNS JONATHAN--74th, Burke County--A.J. & D.W. Orr--24 Feb. 1846--57.5 Acres--145--6--3Cher.

EMBRY ABEL O.--Heards, DeKalb County--26 November 1836--59.25 Acres--176--6--3Cher.

FLOYD ELIJAH--Olivers, Twiggs County--27 March 1837--61 Acres--177--6--3Cher.

SKIPPER BRIGHT--Cravens, Coweta County--15 November 1837--62.75 Acres--208--6--3Cher.

GREAVES JOSEPH D.--602nd, Taliaferro County--30 June 1837--64.5 Acres--209--6--3Cher.

COX FREDERICK--416th, Gwinnett County--7 February 1835--66.5 Acres--240--6--3Cher.

MILLER BRIGHT--Duprees, Washington County--11 November 1835--68 Acres--241--6--3Cher.

HARRIS WEST--Stewarts, Warren County--3 April 1843--70 Acres--272--6--3Cher.

CRITTENDEN JOHN--Coxs, Talbot County--25 April 1840--71.5 Acres--273--6--3Cher.

OWENS ANDREW J.--Braismores, Jones Co.--C.M. Hitchcock--26 March '46--99.5 Acres--290--6--3Cher.

BARNWELL MICHAEL (RS)--Chambers, Houston County--23 Dec. 1843-- 99 Acres--291--6--3Cher.

SMITH GIDEON H. JR.--Smiths, Habersham Co.--18 Sept. 1837--98.5 Acres--292--6--3Cher.

WARWICK JOHN H.--Mullens, Carroll Co.--B.H. Moultree--25 Feb. 1846--97.5 Acres--293--6--3Cher.

McCRIMMON GEORGE--Petersons, Montgomery Co.--4 Dec. 1835--97.25 Acres--294--6--3Cher.

JOINER WILLIAM--121st, Richmond County--3 July 1839--96.75 Acres --295--6--3Cher.

JONES EFFORD L. orphans--Waltzs, Morgan Co.--9 Nov. 1837--96.25 Acres--296--6--3Cher.

TURNER HENRY M.--Russels, Henry County--18 March 1837--95.75 Acres--296--6--3Cher.

TYLER ELIZABETH (WRS)--Prophets, Newton Co.--19 March 1835-- 95.25 Acres--298--6--3Cher.

SMITH JERRYSTONE--Hills, Stewart County--2 April 1836--94.5 Acres--299--6--3Chers.

MARTIN LEVI--242nd, Jackson County--28 November 1835--94 Acres-- 300--6--3Cher.

BOURGER SEABORN--Jones, Morgan County--13 May 1839--93.5 Acres-- 301--6--3Cher.

HUNTER LEONARD C.--Valleaus, Chatham County--31 March 1834--93 Acres--302--6--3Cher.

CROW JOHN W.--Holleys, Franklin Co.--B.H. Moultrie--25 Feb. 1846 --92.5 Acres--303--6--3Cher.

KELLY MARVEL--Stricklands, Meriwether Co.--Wm. Kelly--10 Sept. 1845--36 Acres--304--6--3Cher.

EMFINGER JOHN M.--Not given--1 July 1843--100 Acres--289--6-- 3Cher.

BROWN ELIZABETH widow--Mashburns, Pulaski Co.--24 Mar. 1836--48 Acres--19--12--3Cher.

JOHNSON LUCY H. orphan--Jordans, Bibb County--1 July 1843--48 Acres--20--12--3Cher.

AKRIDGE DAVID soldier--Thomas, Clarke--F.H. Baldwin--6 Feb. 1846 --48 Acres--57--12--3Cher.

GUTHRIE WILLIAM--Atkinsons, Coweta Co.--B.H. Moultire--25 Feb. 1846--48 Acres--58--12--3Cher.

McQUEAN JOHN--Petersons, Montgomery County--13 December 1839-- 48 Acres--95--12--3Cher.

STUBBS JAMES W. & A.F. (orphs)--Bivins, Jones Co.--1 July 1843-- 48 Acres--96--12--3Cher.

SIKES WILLIAM--Browns--Camden County--29 November 1836--48 Acres --133--12--3Cher.

NIX JOHN--Reids, Gwinnett County--15 July 1839--48 Acres--134-- 12--3Cher.

HALL CALEB SR.--Bridges, Gwinnett County--22 March 1843--48 Acres--171--12--3Cher.

MELTON ELI--Levineys, Laurens County--N.P. Harbin--1 Jan. 1846--48 Acres--172--12--3Cher.

LOCKS JOHN orphans--Baileys, Laurens County--19 January 1838--48 Acres--209--12--3Cher.

JONES WILLIAM E.--245th, Jackson County--28 June 1838--48 Acres--210--12--3Cher.

PATERSON P.W.--Willinghams, Harris County--10 April 1838--48 Acres--247--12--3Cher.

McGINNIS JOSEPH L.--Gootes, DeKalb County--8 July 1837--48 Acres--248--12--3Cher.

ALBY WILLIAM--Levitts, Lincoln County--23 December 1835--48 Acres--285--12--3Cher.

LEVERITT JOEL P.--162nd, Greene County--25 Nov. 1842--48 Acres--286--12--3Cher.

NEWTON GILES--Gittens, Fayette County--F.H. Baldwin--6 Feb. 1846--48 Acres--323--12--3Cher.

HAYNES JAMES M.--Mizells, Talbot County--7 November 1840--48 Acres--324--12--3Cher.

ALSOBROOKS AMOS JR.--Sanders, Jones County--18 January 1836--34.75 Acres--361--12--3Cher.

LEWIS ANTONIA--Clietts, Columbia County--4 January 1837--95 Acres--315--14--3Cher.

BIGGARS DAVID--Buck Branch, Clarke County--23 July 1836--91 Acres--316--14--3Cher.

WOOD STERLING--Jordans, Bibb County--3 March 1836--89 Acres--317--14--3Cher.

RABUN JOHN--Bosticks, Twiggs County--2 July 1845--86.5 Acres--318--14--3Cher.

JOURDAINE FLOYD--Stones, Irwin County--1 July 1843--83 Acres--319--14--3Cher.

MEAD THORNTON--McGuires, Gwinnett County--29 March 1837--78.5 Acres--320--14--3Cher.

HOLMES JOHN J.--Haygoods, Washington County--14 February 1837--75 Acres--321--14--3Cher.

WILLIAMS WILLIAM--Barkers, Gwinnett County--1 March 1834--72 Acres--322--14--3Cher.

HENDRICK JAMES J.--Wilsons, Madison County--13 December 1837--68 Acres--323--14--3Cher.

MUNCREAF DAVID--Johnsons, Bibb County--5 August 1839--63 Acres--324--14--3Cher.

SANDERFORD ELEMLICK--Moseleys, Wilkes Co.--14 December 1835--7.26 Acres--1--15--3Cher.

HODGE HARRET (MIN.FAT.ABST.)--McDaniels, Pulaski Co.--1 July '43--55.8 Acres--2--15--3Cher.

TAYLOR JEREMIAH JR.--Whiteheads, Habersham Co.--1 July 1843--54.34 Acres--3--15--3Cher.

SPENCE ALFRED--Nights, Morgan County--19 December 1834--52.54 Acres--4--15--3Cher.

WHITE THOMAS--Mortons, DeKalb Co.--1 July 1843--51.40 Acres--5--15--3Cher.

MAPP MARY (WRS)--160th, Greene County--J. Harwell--6 May 1846--49.92 Acres--6--15--3Cher.

GIBSON SILVANUS--Walkers, Harris County--19 Feb. 1838--48.24 Acres--7--15--3Cher.

PARKERSON JOHN C.--Harts, Jones Co.--J. Harwell--6 May 1846--46.81 Acres--8--15--3Cher.

HUTCHERSON MOSES--Stowers, Elbert County--16 December 1836--45.52 Acres--9--15--3Cher.

GIBSON JOB D.--Hicks, Decatur County--13 December 1838--44.4 Acres--10--15--3Cher.

BROWN REUBEN (orph)--Arringtons, Meriwether Co.--13 Feb. 1841--42.69 Acres--11--15--3Cher.

McGLANN DAVID--Hills, Monroe County--12 Dec. 1837--41.16 Acres--12--15--3Cher.

WILSON JEREMIAH (sol)--Blairs, Lowndes County--7 June 1837--39.68 Acres--13--15--3Cher.

GARNER MOSES SR. (Sol)--Garners, Washington Co.--1 Oct. 1836--38.20 Acres--14--15--3Cher.

FLEMAN JOHN S.--Jenkins, Oglethorpe County--16 May 1837--36.76 Acres--15--15--3Cher.

HALL JAMES--Robinsons, Harris Co.--B.H. Moultrie--25 Feb. 1846--11.25 Acres--16--15--3Cher.

MORAN JOHN B.--Taylors, Putnam County--26 June 1838--49.44 Acres--17--15--3Cher.

DANIEL ISHAM--Sinclairs, Houston County--17 May 1837--48.96 Acres--18--15--3Cher.

SMITH WILLIAM (orph)--Fryers, Telfair County--3 March 1837--48.32 Acres--19--15--3Cher.

CRIM AARON--175th, Wilkes County--24 January 1837--47.64 Acres--20--15--3Cher.

FOWLER JOSHUA--Winters, Jones County--4 Dec. 1834--47.08 Acres--21--15--3Cher.

BROWN JOSHUA--Barkers, Gwinnett Co.--Chas. Day--10 Feb. 1846--46.52 Acres--22--15--3Cher.

CAMPBELL SARAH widow--417th, Walton County--3 March 1837--45.64 Acres--23--15--3Cher.

JOHNSON ROBERT--Smiths, Houston Co.--1 July 1843--44.96 Acres--24--15--3Cher.

BENNETT SOLOMON--Wheelers, Pulaski County--26 March 1840--44.32 Acres--25--15--3Cher.

KENT DANIEL--Bosticks, Twiggs County--30 December 1836--43.64 Acres--26--15--3Cher.

MOORE THOMAS H.--Towers, Gwinnett County--20 December 1839--42.96 Acres--27--15--3Cher.

WATSON ELIZABETH (RS widow)--Murphys, Columbia Co.--1 July 1843--
42.28 Acres--28--15--3Cher.

PURIFOY TILLMAN D.--Groovers, Thomas Co.--J. Lanier--24 Feb.
1846--41.60 Acres--29--15--3Cher.

LUNDY THOMAS (his orphans)--Justices, Bibb Co.--10 Dec. 1853--
40.96 Acres--30--15--3Cher.

STROUD ARCHIBALD L.W.--Smiths, Campbell Co.--7 Sept. 1837--
40.32 Acres--31--15--3Cher.

CHATEEN SARAH widow--Hattons, Baker Co.--19 December 1840--98
Acres--331--22--3Cher.

BAKER NICHOLAS--Wallis, Irwin County--28 October 1839--96 Acres--
332--22--3Cher.

DANIEL LEWIS (Sold)--Crows, Pike Co.--D.E. Bothwell--14 May 1846
--94 Acres--333--22--3Cher.

SCARBOROUGH ALLEN--Baileys, Laurens County--30 June 1343--92
Acres--334--22--3Cher.

PORTER ELIZABETH (WRS)--Doziers, Columbia Co.--D.E. Bothwell--
14 May '46--90 Acres--335--22--3Cher.

SINCLAIRS ROBERT F. (his orphans)--Frasiers, Monroe Co.--9 Nov.
1836--88 Acres--336--22--3Cher.

ANTHONY JOHN--Comptons, Fayette Co.--D.E. Bothwell--14 May 1846--
86 Acres--337--22--3Cher.

McCIBBEN MARGARETT (WRS)--Hoods, Henry County--28 Sept. 1844--
84 Acres--338--22--3Cher.

CLAY SILAS N.--Clintons, Campbell Co.--D.E. Bothwell--14 May
1846--82 Acres--339--22--3Cher.

OGLETREE DAVID--Kindricks, Monroe County--1 July 1843--80 Acres--
340--22--3Cher.

GOOWIN RICHARD--Goodwins, Houston Co.--D.E. Bothwell--14 May
1846--78 Acres--341--22--3Cher.

GROOVER DANIEL--Sewells, Franklin County--12 January 1838--76
Acres--342--22--3Cher.

BUCKNER MILES G.--Kendricks, Putnam County--28 November 1838--
18--25--3Cher.

KING JOHN (R. SOL.)--Liddles, Jackson County--J. Malcom--30
December 1845--19--25--3Cher.

DOLTON JOHN (R. SOL.)--Elsworths, Bibb County--28 April 1838--
80 Acres--54--25--3Cher.

WOOBOTT NOAH--271st, McIntosh County--5 January 1835--55--25--
3Cher.

SINGLETON RICHARD--Stanton, Newton County--1 July 1843--90--25--
3Cher.

BILLINGSBEY MARY widow--702nd, Heard County--23 June 1843--91--
25--3Cher.

DOUGLAS MARY ANN (WID.R.S.)--Arrington, Meriwether Co.--W.B.W.
Dent--31 Mar. 46--126--25--3Cher.

TUCKER NATHAN--Blackshears, Laurens County--19 June 1843--127--
25--3Cher.

THOMAS JOHN S.--Scotts, Baldwin County--24 May 1843--162--25--3Cher.

MEDLOCK JOHN--406th, Gwinnett County--10 December 1836--163--25--3Cher.

HUNT JOHN--Heads, Jones County--B.H. Moultrie--20 May 1846--198--25--3Cher.

LEE JOSEPH H.--Candlers, Bibb County--B.H. Moultrie--20 May 1846--80 Acres--199--25--3Cher.

LASSITER JOHN--Greers, Meriwether County--1 July 1843--234--25--3Cher.

HUMPHREYS WILLIAM (orphs)--Rogers, Burke County--(Blank)--80 Acres--235--25--3Cher.

DENNIS MARY widow--307th, Putnam County--1 July 1843--270--25--3Cher.

ALLEN ROBERT--Andersons, Rabun County--1 July 1843--271--25--3Cher.

GREGORY CHARLES (sol)--Silmans, Pike Co.--William H. Culpepper--26 Jan. 1849--306--26--3Cher.

PERMINTER WILLIAM (soldier)--Allens, Monroe County--30 November 1840--307--15--3Cher.

THOMAS SEPTIMUS--119th, Richmond County--13 November 1841--308--25--3Cher.

THOMPSON NATHAN--146th, Greene County--27 June 1840--309--25--3Cher.

NOLEN ELIZABETH widow--Bakers, Liberty County--9 June 1843--310--25--3Cher.

LEWIS AARON--Jones, Morgan County--20 December 1838--312--25--3Cher.

BINNION ROBERT B.--101st, Hancock County--1 July 1843--313--25--3Cher.

PARR CHARLES D.--Footes, DeKalb County--17 June 1836--314--25--3Cher.

HARREL SARAH widow--Alexanders, Jefferson Co.--J. Malcom--30 Dec. 1845--315--25--3Cher.

ENGLISH JAMES--Burnetts, Lowndes County--19 December 1839--316--25--3Cher.

DOUGLASS ROBERT--Morrisons, Appling County--14 April 1836--317--25--3Cher.

McMICHAEL SILAS--Berrys, Butts County--19 September 1837--318--25--3Cher.

RUNNELS TERRY--Luncefords, Wilkes County--Joseph Watters--12 November 1845--319--25--3Cher.

WILLIAMS CHARLES G.--Mashburns, Pulaski County--16 January 1841--320--25--3Cher.

BRIDGERS JAMES (orphs)--Prescotts, Twiggs County--19 January 1839--321--25--3Cher.

WALLICE JESSE--Johnsons, DeKalb County--19 November 1839--322--25--3Cher.

DUPREE JAMES--Peacocks, Washington County--25 January 1838--323--25--3Cher.

OLIVER PETER M.--Mercks, Hall County--22 March 1843--324--25--3Cher.

NOWLIN DAVID--242nd, Jackson County--12 February 1838--34 Acres--18--27--3Cher.

DAUGGOR NATHANIEL--Rhodes, DeKalb County--25 September 1834--34 Acres--19--27--3Cher.

DOLLAR WILLIAM--Nesbets, Newton County--3 November 1838--34 Acres--54--27--3Cher.

PERRY ALLEN--574th, Early County--17 June 1842--34 Acres--55--27--3Cher.

GARRISON JOHN B.--2nd Section, Cherokee County--1 July 1843--34 Acres--90--27--3Cher.

MOULTRIE JOHN B.--34th, Scriven County--16 December 1840--34 Acres--91--27--3Cher.

FLINGS JOHN (orphs)--Jones, Wilkes County--1 November 1847--34 Acres--126--27--3Cher.

FIELDER JOHN J.--Allisons, Pike Co.--W.F.C. Smith--10 Sept. 1845--34 Acres--127--27--3Cher.

SHAW WILLIAM--Johnsons, DeKalb Co.--P.W. Kilgore--12 January 1846--34 Acres--162--27--3Cher.

WHITHURSTS LANFAIR (orphs)--Coxs, Talbot County--8 May 1843--34 Acres--163--27--3Cher.

DEEN MARTIN--Morrisons, Appling County--7 May 1839--34 Acres--198--27--3Cher.

HERRIN ELIZABETH (Lunatic)--Heards, Butts County--No date--34 Acres--199--27--3Cher.

TILLET LEAH widow--Millers, Ware Co.--B.H. Moultrie--13 Feb. 1846--34 Acres--234--27--3Cher.

FURLOWS CHARLES(orphs)--Cleggs, Walton County--9 July 1850--34 Acres--235--27--3Cher.

EDMONDS WINNEY (W.R.S.)--Luncefords, Wilkes Co.--13 Dec. 1838--34 Acres--270--27--3Cher.

JOINES EDWARD W.--Williams, Washington County--27 August 1839--34 Acres--271--27--3Cher.

GARRETT ELIJAH--Norris, Monroe County--25 September 1834--34 Acres--306--27--3Cher.

CURBOW ELIJAH--Smiths, Campbell County--1 October 1844--34 Acres--306--27--3Cher.

CAMP ROBERT B. (soldier)--Reids, Gwinnett Co.--7 December 1837--98 Acres--325--27--3Cher.

GOGINS JOHN F.--466th, Monroe County--9 March 1837--98 Acres--326--27--3Cher.

HANNAH RICHARD--Hannahs, Jefferson County--23 December 1836--98 Acres--327--27--3Cher.

FITZJERREL BLAKE--Newbys, Jones County--31 May 1843--98 Acres--328--27--3Cher.

MILLER WILLIAM--Harps, Stewart Co.--W.B.W. Dent--31 March 1846--98 Acres--329--27--3Cher.

MIXON JESSE--260th, Scriven County--W.B.W. Dent--31 March 1846--98 Acres--330--3Cher.

WINNINGHAM ABEL--Hamiltons, Gwinnett County--9 July 1836--98 Acres--331--27--3Cher.

DORHERTY ELIZABETH (W.R.S.)--Says, DeKalb County--9 Dec. 1841--98 Acres--332--27--3Cher.

SANFORD CHARLES--Lesters, Monroe County--7 March 1837--98 Acres--333--27--3Cher.

ROSY GASPER--Clelands, Chatham County--25 December 1837--98 Acres--334--27--3Cher.

HARRISON BENJAMIN--Hearns, Butts County--23 January 1838--98 Acres--335--27--3Cher.

WOOLSEY WILLIAM--Hills, Baldwin County--15 December 1837--98 Acres--336--27--3Cher.

BABB WM. (Sol. Ind. War)--Deans, DeKalb Co.--W.B. Johnston--12 Feb. 1846--98 Acres--337--27--3Cher.

GRIFFITH WILLIAM--Liddells, Jackson County--1 July 1843--98 Acres--338--27--3Cher.

ZUBER JOSHUA--Halls, Oglethorpe County--25 October 1839--98 Acres--339--27--3Cher.

HAYGOOD AARON--Griffins, DeKalb County--1 July 1843--98 Acres--340--27--3Cher.

BRADFORD ANN widow R.S.)--Robinsons, Putnam Co.--31 July 1844--98 Acres--341--27--3Cher.

FULKS BRANCH P.--Andersons, Wilkes County--1 July 1843--21 Acres--342--27--3Cher.

McREE MARY (W.R.S.)--Barnetts, Clarke County--16 November 1840--20 Acres--18--28--3Cher.

GRIFFIN JAMES--Crows, Pike County--27 April 1837--20 Acres--19--28--3Cher.

ESPY JAMES (R.S.)--Buck Branch. Clarke County--1 July 1843--20 Acres--54--28--3Cher.

MAHAFFEY HIRAM--Hendons, Carroll County--26 June 1837--20 Acres--55--28--3Cher.

VAUGHN JOHN JUNR.--72nd, Burke County--C. Day--10 February 1846--20 Acres--90--28--3Cher.

HOLT HINES (S.S.)--Cleggs, Walton County--23 November 1838--20 Acres--91--28--3Cher.

THOMPSON JOHN D. (sol.)--Moseleys, Wilkes Co.--24 December 1838--20 Acres--126--28--3Cher.

BRYAN JOHN H.--430th, Upson Co.--W.B. Parker--10 September 1845--20 Acres--127--28--3Cher.

THOMAS ROBERT--466th, Monroe Co.--J.U. Horne--26 February 1846--20 Acres--162--28--3Cher.

LARY WILLIAM J.--Chambers, Gwinnett Co.--W.B. Parker--10 Sept. 1845--20 Acres--163--28--3Cher.

RENFROE JOHN--Manns, Crawford County--23 November 1838--20 Acres --198--28--3Cher.

PAINE WINEFRED (WID.R.S.)--Morris, Crawford Co.--B.H. Moultree--25 Feb. '46--10 Acres--199--28--3Cher.

LAWHORN SIMEON (Sol. late war)--470th, Upson Co.--22 Mar. 1836--20 Acres--234--28--3Cher.

OGILVIE WILLIAM H.--Jenkins, Oglethorpe County--17 April 1838--20 Acres--235--28--3Cher.

HUDMAN WILLIAM F.--Mizells, Talbot Co.--J.U. Horne--26 Feb. 1846 --20 Acres--270--28--3Cher.

STARR JOHN--122D, Richmond County--22 November 1839--20 Acres--271--28--3Cher.

PAINTER EZEKIEL--Dobbs, Hall County--July 1843--20 Acres--306--28--3Cher.

PINKSTON JESSE M.--113th, Hancock County--17 June 1843--20 Acres --307--28--3Cher.

OBANION BRYANT--Blounts, Wilkinson County--2 January 1838--325--11--4Cher.

REID WILLIAM--73rd, Burke County--3 September 1838--326--11--4Cher.

McDOWELL WILLIAM--Stewarts, Jones County--W.B. Johnston--9 May 1846--327--11--4Cher.

HILL GREEN--Bridges, Gwinnett County--W.B. Johnston--9 May 1846--328--11--4Cher.

MILLER JEDIDIAH S. (orphans)--192D, Elbert Co.--No date--64 Acres--329--11--4Cher.

PATRIDGE JAMES--Kendricks, Monroe County--31 December 1838--330--11--4Cher.

HOLSENBAKE WASHINGTON D.--Rhodes, Richmond County--24 November 1836--331--11--4Cher.

DARBY JEREMIAH--Clietts, Columbia County--29 June 1843--332--11--4Cher.

CARTWRIGHT JOHN--141st, Greene County--2 June 1843--333--11--4Cher.

CASE ERMINE--Halls, Butts County--J. Malcom--30 December 1845--334--11--4Cher.

LUMPKIN ROBERT D.--McClains, Newton County--9 December 1835--335--11--4Cher.

STRICKLAND LADDRICK--Allens, Campbell Co.--J.U. Horne--19 Feb. 1846--336--11--4Cher.

PERRY TERRILL (orphans)--Raineys, Twiggs County--9 May 1838--337--11--4Cher.

GREENE JOSEPH F.--Phillips, Talbot County--7 June 1838--338--11--4Cher.

BURKET JOHN--537th, Upson County--17 March 1837--339--11--4Cher.

RED HOLLAND--Bryants, Burke County--16 July 1838--340--11--4Cher.

WILLIAMS ROBERT B.--Moseleys, Wilkes Co.--L.F. Harris--15 Dec. 1846--341--11--4Cher.

WHITTON NICHOLAS--Clevelands, Habersham County--1 December 1835--342--11--4Cher.

MOBLEY SIMPSON P.--Simmons, Crawford County--17 July 1835--88 Acres--288--13--4Cher.

DWITTE LEMUEL--600th, Richmond County--25 February 1836--16 Acres--289--13--4Cher.

ENGLISH JAMES--Burnetts, Lowndes County--19 December 1839--48 Acres--290--13--4Cher.

WRIGHT SAMUEL (sol.)--Martins, Jones County--17 December 1836--76 Acres--291--13--4Cher.

KINNAN AUSTIN--Martins, Washington County--10 March 1834--76 Acres--311--13--4Cher.

REYNOLDS JOHN--Harris, Columbia Co.--L.M. Force--9 February 1846--48 Acres--312--13--4Cher.

SNOW GEORGE W.--Wagnons, Carroll Co.--Spencer Riley--4 Jan. 1846--16 Acres--313--13--4Cher.

BROCKS BENJAMIN (orphans)--74th, Burke County--No date--4 Acres--314--13--4Cher.

WILLIAMS SOLOMON--735th, Troup Co.--E.F. Kinchley--4 October 1850--30 Acres--315--13--4Cher.

JENKINS JOHN--122D, Richmond County--3 July 1839--62 Acres--316--13--4Cher.

DRAKE JAMES V.--Hatchets, Oglethorpe Co.--Chas. Day--12 May 1846--92 Acres--317--13--4Cher.

KENT GUILFORD--Wheelers, Pulaski County--8 March 1834--52 Acres--30--14--4Cher.

HARRISON HENRY--293D, Jasper County--3 April 1834--36 Acres--31--14--4Cher.

YOUNG ORAN W. (orphans)--Evans, Laurens County--21 December 1836--30 Acres--60--14--4Cher.

JOHNSON FRANCIS S.--Candlers, Bibb County--1 July 1843--2 Acres--61--14--4Cher.

GILMORE WILLIAM M.--Robinsons, Harris Co.--Price--16 Feb. 1846--52 Acres--90--14--4Cher.

JOHNSON ARTHUR--Brewers, Monroe County--19 December 1838--36 Acres--117--14--4Cher.

PITTS JOHN D.--Jordons, Bibb County--21 July 1836--30 Acres--118--14--4Cher.

WAGON GEORGE P.--Elsworth, Bibb County--1 July 1843--16 Acres--145--14--4Cher.

WILLIS SUSANNAH (W.R.S.)--168th, Wilkes Co.--24 December 1838--1/2 Acre--146--14--4Cher.

BROWN CHARLES A.--245th, Jackson County--21 April 1843--52 Acres--173--14--4Cher.

SCOTT ASA--Willis, Franklin Co.--W.B. Johnston--12 February 1846--36 Acres--198--14--4Cher.

DIAL TEMPERENCE (H.A.)--Smiths, Madison County--1 July 1843--30 Acres--199--14--4Cher.

HANSON THOMAS K.--693rd, Heard County--1 July 1843--16 Acres--224--14--4Cher.

DAVIS ORANGE--Newbys, Jones County--No date--1/2 Acre--225--14--4Cher.

LEE WILLIAM (his orphans)--Wills, Twiggs County--No date--96 3/4 Acres--49--15--4Cher.

PHILLIPS JOHN--574th, Early County--24 December 1839--72¼ acres--50--15--4Cher.

McCLENDON MOSES J.--364th, Jasper County--15 November 1841--43 3/4 Acres--73--15--4Cher.

WALKER WILLIAM--Hall's, Oglethorpe County--24 May 1841--19 3/4 Acres--74--15--4Cher.

VAUGHAN THOS.--404th, Gwinnett County--No date--1/4 acre--97--15--4Cher.

WIMBERLY EZEKIEL (soldier)--Pounds, Twiggs Co.--26 Mar. 1842--77 3/4 Acres--119--15--4Cher.

DEADWYLER HENRY R.--Wilhites, Elbert Co.--14 December 1836--48 3/4 Acres--120--15--4Cher.

HARALSON ABNER--Nights, Morgan County--19 February 1835--14½ Acres--141--15--4Cher.

JACKSON CLARISSA widow--Bishops, Henry Co.--28 July 1842--79¼ Acres--162--15--4Cher.

GREENE ROGER--248th, Jackson County--23 November 1838--48½ Acres--181--15--4Cher.

HUFF JAMES (ORP. SOL. IND. WAR)--Greens, Oglethorpe Co.--24 Nov. 1842--20 Acres--182--15--4Cher.

HUFF HENRY (ORP. SOL. IND. WAR)--Greens, Oglethorpe Co.--24 Nov. 1842--20 Acres--182--15--4Cher.

CURRY HUGH (his orphans)--Smiths, Wilkinson County--No date--3/4 Acre--201--15--4Cher.

NEACE GEORGE SR. (R.S.)--9th, Effingham Co.--Obed Thompson--8 May '46--81 3/4 Acres--15--18--4Cher.

WILLIAMS JEREMIAH M.--Griffins, Fayette Co.--19 November 1838--53½ Acres--28--18--4Cher.

COWART CULLEN--49th, Emanuel County--S.T. Beecher--8 May 1846--28½ Acres--29--18--4Cher.

LANE ELIZABETH widow--Stantons, Newton Co.--12 Nov. 1836--101½ Acres--53--18--4Cher.

BROWN MARY H. widow--1st, Chatham County--14 June 1843--74 Acres--54--18--4Cher.

MECOMBS WILLIAM--Mimms, Fayette Co.--18 August 1842--45 Acres--65--18--4Cher.

HAMILTON ROBERT--Hamiltons, Hall County--C. Day--9 May 1846--16 Acres--66--18--4Cher.

OWENBY WILLIAM (orphans)--Phillips, Jasper Co.--5 October 1837--93 Acres--86--18--4Cher.

McDONALD NORMAN--Crows, Meriwether Co.--16 December 1836--86½ Acres--87--18--4Cher.

GARRISON CALE (S. late war)--Garners, Coweta Co.--F.T. Polhill--
16 June 1851--36.5 Acres--96--18--4Cher.

LANKFORD JAMES--Millers, Ware County--No date--2 Acres--97--18--
4Cher.

SATTERFIELD LARKIN--Jones, Habersham County--23 February 1836--
84 Acres--113--18--4Cher.

McGEHEE JOHN WILSON--Taylors, Jones County--16 July 1835--50
Acres--114--18--4Cher.

MAYOR DANIEL--Thomas, Clarke County--M. Whitfield--8 May 1846--
28 Acres--121--18--4Cher.

HARRIS EBENEZER--334th, Wayne County--14 January 1836--3.5 Acres
--122--18--4Cher.

BUTLER FORD (soldier)--Griffins, Meriwether Co.--4 May 1836--
102½ Acres--129--18--4Cher.

GARLICKS SAMUEL (orphans)--Roes, Burke County--No date--78 Acres
--134--18--4Cher.

DICKINSON ROGER Q.--606th, Taliaferro County--11 April 1843--
46 Acres--135--18--4Cher.

THOMASON ANDERSON F.--Smiths, Campbell Co.--J.R. Compton--5 Apr.
1854--18 Acres--140--18--4Cher.

GRIMSLEY THOMAS--Tuggles, Meriwether Co.--W.B. Johnston--9 May
'46--94.75 Acres--145--18--4Cher.

MARTIN JAMES V.--145th, Greene Co.--1 July 1843--66.5 Acres--
148--18--4Cher.

MURRILL MARTHA--Valleaus, Chatham County--12 March 1835--39
Acres--149--18--4Cher.

RAY HENRY S.--Johnsons, Bibb County--No date--4 Acres--152--18--
4Cher.

BLOCKER EPHRAIM C.--Hudsons, Marion Co.--Chs. L. Day--12 May
1846--16 Acres--1--19--4Cher.

DORTON JOHN--Gums, Henry County--19 December 1838--84 Acres--41--
19--4Cher.

WOOD MARY (wid.)--Everitts, Washington Co.--B.H. Moultree--12
Feb. '46-- 68 or 36 Acres--42--19--4Cher.

HARRIS WASHINGTON--Jordans, Bibb Co.--J.M. Patton--29 October
1851--49 Acres--61--19--4Cher.

KARR SAMUEL (Sol. Ind. War)--Bowers, Elbert Co.--O.F. Adams--15
Sep. '53--16 Acres--62--19--4Cher.

PURNELL HOPE H.--Athens, Clarke County--C. Day--9 May 1846--42
Acres--116--19--4Cher.

SMITH JOSEPH--Wills, Twiggs Co.--23 August 1838--64 Acres--99--
19--4Cher.

HOOPER JOHN--Gillis, DeKalb County--C. Day--9 May 1846--42 Acres
--116--19--4Cher.

BRADLEY DRURY (orph)--Woods, Morgan County--No date--16 Acres--
117--19--4Cher.

POWELL NOAH--Dilmans, Pulaski County--16 January 1841--92 Acres--
149--19--4Cher.

AUZL JOSEPH--Valleaus, Chatham County--W.B. Johnston--9 May 1846
--68 Acres--150--19--4Cher.

BAKER AARON--561st, Upson County--Henry Phillips--1 May 1846--
42 Acres--165--19--4Cher.

FAY SAMUEL HOWARD--Groces, Bibb Co.--Thompson & Cunningham--26
Feb. 1846--16 Acres--166--19--4Cher.

PITMAN TILMAN R.--Mims, Fayette County--10 January 1834--161--
1--Houston.

WILHITE JOHN M.--Colleys, Madison County--7 April 1837--108--15--
Houston.

EDWARDS SIMEON--Grays, Henry County--5 April 1834--101--8--
Houston.

SHERREN JOHN S. (orphans?)--Luncefords, Wilkes Co.--5 Nov. 1842--
396--16--Henry.

HARDIN BENJAMIN SR.--Doziers, Columbia County--12 March 1836--
244--7--Henry.

RHODES JAMES H.--Grifins, Fayette Co.--23 November 1838--30--17--
Henry.

WALLIS LOVENY widow--Shearers, Coweta County--24 February 1838--
242--7--Henry.

MATTHEWS PHILLIP--494th, Upson County--T.B. Davies--2 January
1847--127--6--Dooly.

BRYAN WILLIAM--Raineys, Twiggs County--2 December 1836--251--6--
Dooly.

SORRELL IRVEN (Sol. 1784 to 1797)--Arringtons, Meriwether Co.--
16 Nov. '35--236--25--Lee.

ROBINSON ALEXANDER E.--Graves, Putnam County--10 November 1841--
214--28--Lee.

REYNOLDS BENJAMIN (sol.)--McMillins, Lincoln Co.--15 Aug. 1834--
220--10--Habersham.

RAY GEORGE--417th, Walton County--11 April 1834--219--4--Muscogee.

THOMAS GEORGE W.--McLins, Butts County--22 December 1837--21--
9--Muscogee.

GATLIN JAMES--113th, Hancock County--25 August 1834--131--16--
Muscogee.

WAY WM. JAMES--15th, Liberty County--28 November 1835--124--21--
Muscogee.

WALLER SARAH (W.R.S.)--Williams, Washington County--5 March 1835
--13--6--Coweta.

NEWBERRY JOHN--Butts, Monroe County--5 January 1837--226--10--
4Cher.

SHIPP CANNON H.--Stantons, Newton Co.--E. Daggett (6 Feb. 1847)--
6 Dec. 1839--143--10--4Cher.

WILDER WILLIAM--Justices, Bibb County--2 January 1838--68--18--
4Cher.

HAMMOND ABNER--Justices, Bibb County--2 January 1838--292--9--
3Cher.

RAMSEY DRURY M.--Smiths, Franklin County--12 March 1836--150--
27--3Cher.

CRAWFORD JOEL--Husons, Baldwin County--3 January 1823--172--4--Early--1820LL.

COX WILLIS--Pittmans, Gwinnett County--10 October 1831--173--4--Early--1820LL.

CURRY WILLIAM--Green's, Greene County--25 October 1828--236--4--Early--1820LL.

JONES JAMES orphs.--Dewetts, Pulaski County--B.S. Jordon--(Blank)--228--7--Early--1820LL.

CLARK DAVID--Floyds, Washington County--28 Aug. 1841--229--7--Early--1820LL.

ANDERS FREDERICK--Carsons, Laurens County--B.S. Jordon--240--7--Early--1820LL.

MATHALL WILLIAM T.--Martins, Jasper County--15 September 1832--251--9--Early--1820LL.

MORTHALL WILLIAM T.--See Mathall--1820LL.

WORTHALL WILLIAM T. See Mathall--1820LL.

REEVES JESSE orp.--Shropshires, Jasper Co.--J.W. Horne--6 Sept. 1842--114--10--Early--1820LL.

WILLIAMSON THOMAS E.--Stewarts, Clark County--20 Aug. 1832--266--14--Early--1820LL.

WILLIAMS JAMES--Phillips, Jasper Co.--21 Apr. 1842--John B. Lamar--122--16--Early--1820LL.

WYNN JOHN P.--Adams, Montgomery--14 November 1829--59--17--Early--1820LL.

ALEXANDER SUSANNAH widow--Jeffersons, Jones Co.--12 Dec. 1831--312--11--Early--1820LL.

RIGGS STEPHEN--De Loachs, Bulloch County--Cary Cox--25 April 1842--119--27--Early--1820LL.

REESE BENJAMIN--Williams, Warren County--24 November 1825--167--28--Early--1820LL.

THOMAS PATRICK M.--Reids, Early County--25 January 1823--3--6--Gwinnett--1820LL.

CLARK LEWIS--Olivers, Jackson County--22 November 1825--342--6--Gwinnett--1820LL.

POTTER RIAL--Whites, Jasper County--25 January 1825--382--7--Gwinnett--1820LL.

STONE JENNCY--Penningtons, Jones County--27 Oct. 1830--42--5--Habersham--1820LL.

MELL THOMAS S.--Mells, Liberty Co.--L. Franklin--21 Apr. 1842--111--12--Habersham--1820LL.

WILKINSON SELAH widow--Hendersons, Morgan Co.--2 Dec. 1826--116--12--Habersham--1820LL.

PETER ABNAH--Penns, Elbert County--C. Attaway--16 May 1842--141--12--Habersham--1820LL.

HADAWAY AULEY widow--Moores, Wilkes County--5 October 1832--159--9--Hall--1820LL.

ADAMS GEORGE--Brantleys, Richmond County--25 September 1825--13--1--Irwin--1820LL.

MILLER JACOB--Mills, Chatham County--14 December 1840--14--1--Irwin--1820LL.

BEAL'S LEVI (orphs)--Griffins, Twiggs Co.--Iverson L. Harris--16 May '49--34--7--Irwin--1820LL.

JORDAN ELIZ. (wid)--Smiths, Jefferson Co.--Iverson L. Harris--16 May '49--7--Irwin--1820LL.

GRACE THOMAS--Palmers, Richmond County--12 December 1823--332--8--Irwin--1820LL.

COAKER ALLEN?--Floyds, Washington County--J.J. Duggan--25 July 1842--37--9--Irwin--1820LL.

WALLIS WILLIAM C.--Wallis, Jasper County--C. Attaway--16 May 1842--385--9--Irwin--1820LL.

DUNAWAY ISSAC--Franklin County--21 December 1825--49--10--Irwin--1820LL.

LUMPKIN SAMUEL--Holtzclaws, Oglethorpe Co.--L.C. Paulett--19 Nov. 1845--313--10--Irwin--1820LL.

LEE ARCHIBALD--Stephens, Baldwin County--21 October 1830--328--10--Irwin--1820LL.

WILLIS KISSIAH widow--McCrarys, Baldwin County--27 Feb. 1837--295--12--Irwin--1820LL.

STUDDARD ABRAHAM--Davis, Walton--23 December 1825--246--13--Irwin--1820LL.

WATTS JOHN--Hairs, Early County--29 October 1835--180--16--Irwin--1820LL.

WALKER DAVID--McPhails, Pulaski County--18 January 1822--239--3--Walton--1820LL.

APPENDIX A

INDEX TO BUYERS OF REVERTED LANDS.

ADAMS: O. F., 38
ALLEN: D., 47
ALLEN: J., 35
ATTAWAY: C., 63, 64
AUSTIN: E., 30
AUSTIN: W. C., 37
BALDWIN: J., 20
BALDWIN: F. H., 51, 52
BANGS: Joseph, 48
BANKS: R., 11
BEECHER: S. T., 60
BERRY: E., 43
BERRY: Ed, 43
BETHUNE: B. T., 05
BETHUNE: J. N., 49
BLACKMAN: J., 38
BLACKMAN: Jas, 38
BLOOM: T. P., 20, 22, 23, 28, 44, 45
BOTHWELL: D. E., 54
BOWEN: Caleb P., 30
BRICE: Joseph, 34
BROWN: Caleb P., 31
BROWN: L., 21
BROWN: T. L., 18
BROWN: W. B., 42
BUARRON: A. S., 42
BURT: Reuben T., 08
BUSCOE?: L. H., 35
CAMPBELL: C., 43
CANDLER: S. C., 34, 35, 36
CANTRELL: J. M., 50
CANTRELL: James, 07
CANTRELL: Jas., 10
CARP: W. A., 07, 28
CARP: W. C., 16
CAPYELL: J.H., 32
CASH: William C., 31
CASTLEBERRY: P., 10, 11
CHERRY: T., 07, 23
CHISHOLM: --, 43, 44
CLAYTON: Stewart, 49
COAL: J. C., 36
COBB: J. M., 07, 47
COGGINS: A. J., 40
COLLINS: M., 24
COMPTON: J. P., 31, 38-41, 46, 47, 61
COMPTON: P. M., 35, 37, 43, 44
CONYERS: W. D., 32, 33, 35, 37
COOPER: J. F., 09
COOPER: L. W., 05, 18, 46
COPYELL: J. H., 31
COPYETT: J. H., 31, 32
COX: Cary, 63
CULPEPPER: William H., 55
CUNNINGHAM: --, 62
CUTLER: P. P., 34, 35
DAGGETT: E., 62
DAVIDSON: W. H., 38
DAVIDSON: Wm. H., 37
DAVIES: T. B., 62
DAVIS: J. W., 36
DAY: C., 18, 25, 29, 30, 37, 41, 57, 60, 61
DAY: Chas., 53, 59
DAY: Chs. L., 61
DAY: Chs., 20
DAY: S. G., 18, 19
DENT: W. B. W., 54, 55
DUGGAN: J. J., 64
EASON: W., 37
ELLIS: Ps.tord, 44
ESKE: N. M., 0
FOSKE: N. M., 59
FOSTER: Ira R., 20
FOSTER: John, 42
FRANKLIN: L., 63
FREEMAN: Fletcher, 48
FUPY: W. R., 45
GAY: S. G., 32
GIBSON: H. A., 43
GOOLSBY: A., 34
GOSS: B. F., 08
GRAHAM: W. C., 07
GRAHAM: W. H., 06
GROVES: Wm. F., 22
HANSELL: W. T., 21
HARBIN: N. P., 52
HARRIS: --, 26, 30, 32, 45
HARRIS: Iverson, 64
HARRIS: L. C., 43, 58
HARRISON: C. C., 41
HARWELL: J., 53
HASON: T. R., 47
HIDE?: Isaac, 06

HITCHCOCK: C. M., 45, 51
HORNE: J. U., 25, 57, 58
HORNE: J. W., 63
HORNE: S. W., 01
HYDE: F. P., 06
HYDE: James, 08
JACKSON: D. M., 46
JOHNSON: J. C., 22, 24
JOHNSON: T. D., 37
JOHNSON: W. B., 31, 33
JOHNSON: W. P., 31
JOHNSTON: W. B., 25, 42, 45, 57-59, 61, 62
JOHNSTON: Wm. B., 42, 44, 45
JONES: Timothy, 26
JORDON: B. S., 63
KEES: T. B., 49
KEITH: G., 13
KEITH: Geo., 13
KELLOGG: Geo., 17
KELLY: Wm., 51
KILGORE: P. W., 56
KINCHLEY: E. F., 59
KINCHLEY: Edward F., 44
KINGSBURY: G., 38
LANIER: J., 54
LEE: S. W., 14, 44
LEWIS: B., 34
LOGAN: F., 20, 21
LOOPER: J. W., 06
MALCOM: J., 54, 55, 58
MARTIN: William, 07
MCCLUNG: W. W., 37
MCCLURE: J. A., 11
MILLEN: --, 30, 32, 45
MILLEP: --, 26
MITCHELL: Thos., 21
MOCK: Henry, 46
MOORE: J. A., 37
MOULTREE: B. H., 51, 58, 61
MOULTRIE: B. C., 31
MOULTRIE: B. H., 23, 28, 31-34, 36, 39, 53, 55, 56
NICHOLS: W. P., 48
ORR: A. J., 18, 20, 50
ORR: D. W., 18, 20, 50
PAINE: W. W., 31, 38-41, 46
PALMORE: A., 12, 13
PALMORE: J. D., 12
PARKER: W. B., 14, 19-21, 49, 57
PAPP: J., 05
PATTERSON: Saml., 17
PATTON: J. M., 61
PAULETTI: L. C., 64
PHILLIPS: H., 06
PHILLIPS: Henry, 62
POLHILL: F. T., 61
PPICE: --, 59
RANDOLPH: A., 13
RICHARDSON: J. S., 30, 47
RILEY: S., 25, 28
RILEY: Spenser, 25, 39-41, 59
ROBERTS: Jesse, 36
SANDS: J. A., 02, 19, 22
SIMMONS: W., 42
SIMMONS: Wm. S., 42
SMITH: J. H., 07
SMITH: J. N., 31
SMITH: John, 07
SMITH: John, Jr., 10
SMITH: W. F. C., 56
STEPHENS: Mary, 50
TALLEY: J., 13
TAZY: Piddle, 30
TERHUNE: A. C., 42
THOMAS: E., 15
THOMPSON: --, 62
THOMPSON: Jno. Jr., 37
THOMPSON: M. S., 06
THOMPSON: Obed, 60
THOMPSON: W. S., 28
TISON: B., 42
TURMAN: Joel C., 43
TURNER: J., 11
WALKER: W. G., 41
WALTHALL: --, 43, 44
WATTERS: Joseph, 55
WHITFIELD: M., 61
WILLIAMS: J. B., 36
WILLINGHAM: H., 20, 31
WILSON: Orphny, 05
WOOD: J., 38
WRIGHT: W. J., 43
WYNN: A. B., 01

AARON: William Riley, 46
ADAMS: David, Sr., 42; George, 63; Hezekiah, 47; John, 02
ADCOCK: Anderson W., 27
AKENS: Samuel, 44
AKINS: Catlett J., 16
AKRIDGE: David, soldier, 51
ALBY: William, 52
ALEXANDER: James S., 16; Susannah, widow, 63
ALLEN: Cyrus, 04; James L., 28; John W., 43; Joseph, 10; Robert, 55; William H., 21; William M. B., 09
ALLMAN: John, 13
ALSOBROOKS: Amos, Sr., 52
ANDERS: Frederick, 63
ANDERSON: George T., 26; James, 10; John, 42; Sterling, his orphans, 39
ANDREWS: Garnett, 27; Joseph, 38
ANTHONY: John M., 33; John, 54; Micaiah, 16
ARMSTRONG: Martin, 42
ARNOLD: Elizabeth, widow, 24; John, 42; Wesley, 24; William, 02
ASBEL:
ASHWORTH: Joseph, 45; Job, 09
ASKEW: Perry, 43
ATKINSON: Lazarus, Sr., 34
AUL: Joseph, 62
AVERY: Jonathan, 16
AYRES: Larkin C., 13
BABB: Wm. (Sol. Ind. War), 57
BADOLET: Mary, widow, 41
BAGGETT: John, 46
BAILEY: Hezekiah, 50; Julian, 24
BAIN: Emnor, 42
BAKER: Aaron, 62; Abner, 05; Dennis B., 14; Hugh, 21; John M.C.L., 21; Nicholas, 54
BARBER: McGilbrey, 47
BARBIN: Arthur, 07
BARKSDALE: John, 17
BARNES: John R., 29
BARNETT: Calvin, 08; William, 18, 44
BARNWELL: Michael (RS), 51
BAPROW: William, Jr., 02
BAPTLEMAN: John W., 19
BARTON: Wm., 14
BASS: Howel R., 02
BATES: Napoleon B., 25
BATTEY: Joseph S., 30
BATTLE: Joseph A., 14
BATTS: McAllen, 28; William, 18
BAUGHN: Willarg H., 26
BAXTER: John, 09
BEADLES: Sarah (WRS), 49
BEALL: James B., 31
BEAL SI: Levi, (orphs.), 64
BEALL: Alexander R., 06; Alpheus, 38
BFALLE: John W., 37
BEANCHAMP: John, 02
BEARD: James A., Sr., 46; William M., 49
BEASLEY: Cynthia, widow, 48
BEATY: James, 13
BECKHAM: Laban, 38
BELCHER: Philip, 14
BELL: Thomas, 08
BENJAMIN: Margaret, widow, 26
BENNETT: Christopher G., 16; Solomon, 53
BENTLEY: John, 21
BERRY: Andrew J., 13
BEST: Jacob C., 32
BETTERTON: William, 06
BEVERLE: John, 22
BIGGARS: David, 52
BILLINGSLEY: Mary, widow, 54
BILLINGSLEA: James F., 17
BINION: Wiley H., 23
BINNION: Robert B., 55
BIRD: Bellings Britt, 37; George L., 15
BINSONG: Parris M., 33
BISSELL: Leonard, 50
BLACK: Samuel, Sr., 06
BLACKWELL: James B., 05
BLAFEY: Council, 38; David, Sr., 23
BLALOCK: John H. orphan, 48; Reuben, 36
BLEDSOE: Benjamin, 41
BLOCKER: Ephraim C., 61
BOGGASS: Jeremiah, 41
BOGGS: Archibald, 58
BOHANNAN: Budda, 20
BOLECLAIR: Lewis A. L., 15
BOLEN: George, his orphans, 23; Roda, widow, 34
BONDURANT: Josiah, 23
BONNER: James, 03; Josiah M., 42
BOSTWICK: Charles H., 28
BOSWORTH: Sarah, widow, 37
BOTTOMS: Burrell, 47
BOULS: Nelson, 25
BOURGER: Seaborn, 51
BOWDOIN: Josiah, 50
BOWEN: Nancy, widow, 21
BOWER: Jonathan, 13

BOYD: George, 17
BOYKIN: Henry, 12
BRACEY: William, 05
BRACKETT: John, 17
BRADBURG: Joseph, 15
BRADEN: Elias, 46
BRADFORD: Ann, Widow R. S., 57
BRADLEY: Drury (orph), 61; Pressley, William D., 08
BRADY: Alfred, 12
BRAMBLETT: John, 18
BRANHAM: Wiley, 26
BRASWELL: Benjamin, 23; Blaney, 27
BRAWNER: Henry S., 02; William, 04
BRAZIEL: Warren H., 29
BRAZILE: Elizabeth, wid., 08
BREWER: Elizabeth, widow, 21
BRIDGERS: James, (orphs.), 55
BRIDGES: Bennett, 39; Howell, 20
BRITT: Henry, 20
BROCK: John J., 37
BROCKS: Benjamin (orphans), 59
BROOKS: Elijah, 35; Felix, 10; Isham, 18; John, 49
BROWN: Charles A., 59; Edward, 43; Elizabeth, widow, 51; Hugh, 28; John D., 03, 04; Joshua, 53; Mary H., widow, 60; Reuben, orph, 53; Samuel B., 45; William, 27
BROWNING: Edmond, 14; Margaret (Wrs), 49; Young H., 26
BRUMBELO: James, 06
BRYAN: George W., 34; John H., 41, 57; John, 24; Samuel J., 03; William, 26
BRYANT: Wiley, 09
BUCHANNAN: Benjamin B., 08; Isaac, 11
BUCKNER: Henry M., 23; Miles G., 54
BURCH: Charles, 11
BURKE: John, 58
BURKS: Wiley P., 06
BUNAM: William, Jr., 41
BUPNETT: Isaac Sr., 38; Joseph, 43; Thomas, 08
BURNSIDE: Eleanor wid., 05
BUSBY: Nathan, 30
BUSH: Allen, 32
BUSTIN: William, 24
BUTLER: Ford, (soldier), 61; John, 08
BUTTS: William N., 35
BYNUM: Reason, 16
CABOS: John, 04
CADE: Drury, 40
CALDWELL: Whitfield, 14
CALLIER: Joseph A., 44
CALVIN: John, 12
CAMAK: James, 25
CAMP: John, 24; Robert B., (soldier), 56; Russell, 36
CAMPBELL: Charter, 28; Sarah, wid., 53
CANNON: Elizabeth, widow, 21
CARLEE: John, 26
CARR: John, 06
CARRUTHERS: James, 29
CARSON: James J., 03
CARSTARPHEN: Thomas C., 42
CARTER: John D., 12; Pendleton, 07; Thomas J., 03
CARTWRIGHT: John, 58
CARUTHERS: Jane L., widow, 44
CASE: Ermine, 58
CASEY: Parris P., 13
CASON: Joseph, 36
CASON: John, Jr., 29
CASSELL: James, 23
CAWTHEN: James, 39; Samuel, 15
CHALMERS: John M., 33
CHAMBERLAIN: James, 31
CHAMBERS: Wilson, 24
CHANDLER: Robert, soldier, 48
CHAPPELL: Jefferson, 07; Obadiah, 13
CHARLTON: Thomas U. P., 19
CHASTAIN: John, 15; Jonathan D., 15
CHATEEN: Sarah, widow, 54
CHATFIELD: Isaac, orphan, 34
CHERRY: William B., 50
CHESSER: Mathew, 40
CHILDS: Benjamin, 36
CHITWOOD: Pleasant, 19
CHRISTAIN: Gideon, 19
CLARK: David, 63; John M., 37; Lewis, 63; Thomas J., 32
CLAY: Silas N., 04
CLEMANS: Mary M., widow, 48
CLEMONS: William, 29
CLIFTON: Ballew C., 43
CLINTON: Wm. P., 11
COAKER: Allen J., 64
COAL: Isaac, 08
COCHRAN: James, 27; Cheadle, 41
COGBURN: John A., 30
COINS: John, 47
COLVIN: John, 47
COLLAR: William, 09
COLLINS: John, 33
COLQUITT: Benjamin, 41
CONE: Stephen, 40
CONNELLY: William, 44

CONNER: John, 16; Wilson, 09; Zephaniah F., 24
COODY: William G., 42
COOK: Beverly C., 10; John, Jr., 32; Joshua, 36
COOPER: David, 45
COOTS: John, 40
COPE: Adam, 17
COPP: Belton R., 37
COPPIDGE: Charles, 09
CORREY: Thomas, 15
COVINGTON: Sally, widow, 34
COWARD: William, 05
COWART: Cullen, 60
COWEN: Robert, 18
COX: Frederick, 50; Wiley J., 23; Willis, 63
CRAIG: Elbert E., 49
CRAMER: Joseph, 45
CRAWFORD: Arthur, 03; Charles, 21; Joel, 63
CREEPMAY: Rebecca (Wrs), 49
CRIM: Aaron, 53
CRITTENDEN: John, 50
CROCKETT: James W., 02
CROSS: James Jr., 43
CROSSLEY: Edward, 41
CROUCH: George, 01
CROW: John W., 51
CRUMPTON: Thomas, 21
CRUTCHFIELD: Stapleton, 10
CULBERT: Thomas, 44
CUMMING: John, 33
CUPBOW: Elijah, 56
CURRY: Hugh, (his orphans), 60; William, 63
D'XON: Mordecai S., 24
DABOUVILLE: Joseph, 15
DANELY: Sarah, widow, 16
DANIEL: Isham, 53; Lewis, (Sol.), 54; Reuben E., 40; William B., 36
DARBY: Jeremiah, 58
DARDEN: Abner, 32
DARSEY: Pezin, 49
DASHER: Cristian H., 39; Thomas, 41
DAUGDOP: Nathaniel, 56
DAVIDSON: James, 52
DAVIS: Adam, 09; Charles, 35; Gardner H., 21; Jesse H., 41; John, 10; Orange, 60
DAWSON: James, orp., 47
DEADWYLER: Henry R., 60
DEAN: George, 39; James, 30
DEATON: William, Jr., 08
DEEN: Martin, 56
DELAIGH: Nicholss, 38
DELCESSILIM: Wm. E., 45
DELONY: Robert J., 29
DEPPY: Lawrence, 30
DENNIS: Mary, widow, 55
DENSON: Pichard, 06
DEWBEPPY: William, 06
DIAL: Martin, Sr., 04; Temperance, (H. A.), 59
DICKINSON: Jand. orphans, 38; Poner Q., 61; Wiley, 01
DICKSON: Charles A., 45; John, 05
DIFERNATTEE: Reuben, R., 02
DINON: William T., 18
DINDY: Youngsett, 10
DOLLAR: William, 56
DOLTON: John (R. Sol.), 54
DOOLY: Clement, 11
DORHERTY: Elizabeth, (W.R.S.), 57
DORSON: John, 61
DOUGLAS: Mary Ann, (Wid. R. S.), 54
DOUGLASS: John, 14, 15; Robert M., 39; Robert, 55
DOWNEP: Joseph, 33
DPAIT: James V., 52; Samuel, 28
DUBERRY: Thomas, 25
DUGAS: Vincendieve, 18
DUKE: Green R., 31; John T., 07
DUNAGAN: Joshua, 26
DUNAWAY: Isaac, 64
DUNKIN: Peter, Sr., 31
DUNN: James H., 45
DUPREE: Burges, 08; James, 56
DURAN: Jesse, 13
DURDEN: Lewis, 41
DURHAM: Seabon J., 07; Thomas, his orphans, 14
DWELL: Lemuel, 13
DWITTE: Lemuel, 59
DYAL: Lyiphie, widow, 16
EASTEPS: Sarah, widow, 26
ECHOLS: Elijah V., 09
ECKLES: Thomas, orphans, 13
EDENFIELD: David, Sr., 36
EDMONDS: Winney (W.R.S.), 56
EDMONDSON: Daniel, 22; James, 37; James, Sr., 19
EDWARDS: Alfred, Sr., 14; Berry, 40; Littleton C., 33; Robert L., 25; Simeon, 62
ELDERS: William N. orphans, 28
ELLIOTT: Larkin M., (his orphans), 48; Martha, widow, 40; William, 14

ELLIS: James, Jr., 46; William, 14
ELSBERRY: Lindsey, 18
EMBRY: Abe C., 50
EMBDUS: Elizabeth, widow, 42
ENFINGER: John M., 51
ENGLISH: James, 55, 59
ESPY: James, (R.S.), 57
ETHREDGE: Enoc, 12
ETHRIDGE: Joseph S., 43
EUBANKS: John, Sr., 05
EVANS: Arden, his orphans, 14; Jesse, Jr., 25
EVERETT: James A., 15; Solomon, 44
EVERITT: Thomas, 33
FALKNER: James W., 35
FAPIS: William, 07
FAPMER: Isham, 46
FARR: Marv. Wid., 07
FAY: Samuel Howard, 62
FEARS: Ezekiel, 13
FEATHERSTON: William, 22
FELTON: Hartwell, 16
FERGUSON: Isaac, 01
FEW: Ignatious A., Sr., 14
FIELDER: John J., 56
FIELDS: Delilah, widow, 48
FILGRIM: Mitchell, Sr., 30
FINCHER: Joshua, 30
FINDEY: William, 20
FINLEY: Allen, 18
FITZJERREL: Blake, 56
FLANIGAN: Kenjan, 32
FLEMAN: John S., 53
FLEMING: Samuel, 38
FLEMMING: Robert, 27
FLINGS: John (orphs), 56
FLOURNOY: Simon, 3
FLOYD: Elijah, 50
FOAPD: James A., 40
FORD: Marjam, 19
FORRESTER: George B., 02
FORT: Charles M., 04
FOWLER: Joshua, 63
FULKS: Branch P., 57
FULLER: Benjamin F., 21
FUSON: Samuel, 48
FURGERSON: Burrel, 34
F.PLOW: Osborn S., 22
F.PLOWS: Charles, (orphs), 56
GAINER: Samuel, 3
GAINS: Ann T., widow, 22
GALLAWAY: John, 19
GALLOWAY: James, 03
GANES: Cooper, 11
GAPDNEP: Starling, 49
GAPLICKS: Samuel (orphans), 61
GARNEP: John N., 05; Moses, Sr. (sol.), 53
GARPER: Elijah, 56; Jonn, 26; Joseph, 45
GARR.SON: Cale (S. late war), 61; John B., 56
GATLIN: James, 62
GATEWAY: Jonn, 17
GAMS: Sampson, 11
GIBSON: Job D., 53; Nelson, 19; Samuel, 15; Silvanus, 53
GIDDEN: Frederick M., 48
GI.BEPT: Thomas W., 44
GILLISPIE: John P., 04
GILMORE: William M., 59
GIVILLE: Margaret, 30
GLOVEP: John, 03
G.VATEP: John, 34
GODOAPD: John, 38
GODFREY: Freeman, 43
GOOD: Alexander, 17
GODWIN: Richard, 54
GORDAY: Elijah, 47
GOPDEN: John, 42
GORDON: Alexander J., 20
GP.MAS: John, 17; Thomas, 64
GP.HAS: Allen, 44
GRAINGEP: John D., 25
CRANBERPY: Sam M., 50
GRAVES: Solomon, 08
GPAY: John M., 33; Marv. wid., 10; Patterson, 36
GP.EEN: Joseph D., 50
GREEN: Alexander S., 40; Roger, 24
GREENE: Joseph F., 58; Roger, 60
GREEP: Robert, 26
GREGORY: Charles (sol), 55
GP.ESHAM: Jeremiah, 29
GP.FFIN: James, 57; John, 20; S. Bennett, 36
GPIFFITH: Henry W., 24; William, 57
GRIMSLEY: Thomas, 61
GP.OCEL: James, 11
GPOOVEP: Daniel, 54
GPOVES: John W., 25
GUESS: William, 07
GUNN: James, 12; Larkin R., 12
GUTHRIE: William, 51
HADAWAY: Auley, widow, 63
HAGAN: Isom, 24
HAIL: John, 20
HAISTEN: Harrison, 32

HALL: Caleb, Sr., 52; Dempsey, 33; James, 53; Thomas L., 29; William, 24
HAMBY: William, Sr., 19
HAMILTON: Robert, 60
HAMLET: Sanders W., 14
HAMMOCK: Asa A., 38; Jeremiah, 38
HAMMOND: Aaron, 62
HAN: Ichabod, 22
HANN: William, 09
HANNAH: Richard, 56
HANSON: Thomas K., 60
HARALSON: Abner, 60
HARDEN: James, his orphans, 23
HARDIN: Benjamin B., 46; Benjamin, Sr., 62
HARDMAN: Allen, 20
HARFORD: William, 47
HARGRAVE: Bright H., 50
HARGROVES: George, Sr., 28
HARP: Edward, 03
HARPER: George, 20
HARREL: Sarah, widow, 55
HARRELL: Rodham, 34
HARRINGTON: Moses, 25
HARRIS: Albert B., 48; Alexander F., 12; Alsey J., wid., 11; Churchwell, his orphans, 41; Ebenezer, 61; Hannah, wid., 08; Nathan, 20; Nathaniel, 11; Wesley, 41; West, 50; William, 45
HARRISON: Benjamin, 57; George, 24; Henry, 59; Tilman, 32
HARVEY: Albert G., 07; Emanuel, 10
HARVIL: Ellis, 29
HARWELL: John, 43
HARY: William, 27
HASELETT: John, 08
HASTING: Benjamin, 03
HATCHER: William, 29
HATHCOCK: Middleton, 20
HAVENER: William, 48
HAWKINS: Benjamin, 11; Edward, 22; Nicholas, 43
HAWTHORN: Jonathan C., 04
HAYDOOD: Aaron, 57
HAYMANS: Elisha, 28
HAYNES: James M., 52; Johnson, 32
HEAD: James A., 27; James B., 32
HEFLIN: Johnson, 13
HENDERSON: Samuel R., 16
HENDERLY: James B., 52
HENDRICKS: Gilliford E., 50
HENDRIX: John, 21
HENDRY: Ann, widow, 19
HENLY: William, 35
HERBION: Benjamin, 25
HERRIN: Elizabeth, 56
HERRINGTON: Henry, 49
HICKLIN: Elizabeth wid., 05
HICKS: Samuel, 15
HIGASON: William, 35
HIGGINBOTHAM: Nelson, 11
HILL: Elizabeth, widow, 33; Green B., 25; Green, 58; Robert H., his orphans, 23; Wald, 19
HILLSMAN: Pascal W., 34
HINES: Howell, 20; James, 07
HINKLE: Solomon, 31
HOBBS: William H., 02
HODGE: Harret (Min. Pat. Abst.), 52
HODGES: Augustus G. W., 49; Nancy, wid., 08
HODNETT: Benjamin,(Head of family), 45
HOLCOMB: Thomas, 03
HOLDEN: Thomas, 16
HOLLAND: Tobias, 34
HOLMES: James P., 17; John J., 52; Sharick, 21
HOLSENBAKE: Washington D., 58
HOLT: Hines (S.S.), 57
HOLTON: Elizabeth, widow, 47
HOMES: Asenberry, 12
HOOD: Ichabod, 12
HOOKS: William, 12
HOOPER: John, 61; Johnson M., 48
HOOTEN: James, 45
HOOTON: Bedford, 49
HOPPER: Sarah, widow, 39
HORISE: Nathan, 20
HORN: Isaac, 12; Whitington, 02
HOUSE: Elias, 46; Zachariah B., 07
HOWARD: James W., 35; John H., 37
HOWELL: Isaac, 20; William, 02
HOWPARD: John S., 33
HUCKABY: James, 20
HUDGINS: James, 46; Josiah, 40
HUDMAN: William F., 58
HUDSON: William, orphans, 06
HUFF: Henry, (Orp. Sol. Ind. War), 60; James, (Orp Sol. Ind. War), 60
HUGHES: Littleberry, 45; William L., 44
HUGHLERY: William, 11
HUGIENIN: Edward H., 40
HULL: Thomas, Sr., 18
HUMPHREYS: William (orphs.), 55
HUNT: John, 55

HUNTER: Leonard C., 51
HUTCHERSON: Moses, 53
HUTCHINSON: James G., 10
INGE: Charles, 35
INGRAM: John, orphs., 49; William P., 48
IVEY: Charles, 39
IVY: Ephraim Sent., 01
JACKSON: Clarissa, widow, 60; Edmund, 01; James A., 08
JAMES: Ebenezer, 34
JARNION: Emery, 37
JARRARD: Josiah D., 28
JARRETT: James, 12
JEFFRIES: Drewry, 14
JENKINS: John, 59; Reason, 29; Thomas, 11
JOHNS: Jonathan, 50
JOHNSON: Arthur, 59; Bryant, 08; Darius, 27; David, 26; Elijah, 01; Francis S., 59; Henry, 05; James, 46; Lucy H., orphan, 51; Martin, 41; Philip, 42; Robert, 53; Surywood B., 29; William, 28
JOINER: Peter, 41; William, 51
JOINES: Edward W., 56
JONES: Anthony, 48; David G., 16; Efford L., orphs., 51; Elizabeth, (Widow),03; Ephraim, 07; James H., Jr., 14; James, (orphs.), 63; Jesse, 22; Moses, 33; Stephen, 37; Wiley, 37; William (Soldier), 46; William B., 32; William E., 52; Willis B., 33
JORDAN: Elias, 08; Eliz, (wid), 64; Elizabeth, wid., 11; William D., 18
JOURDAINE: Floyd, 52
JUSTISE: John H. R., 36
KARR: Samuel, (Sol. Ind. War), 61
KEENER: Henry, 16
KEITH: Asa, 23
KELLY: Marvel, 51; Terrell, 39
KENDRICK: Jacob B., 12; James R., 39; Jones, 13
KENNAMORE: David, 02
KENNEDY: John C., 35
KENT: Daniel, 53; Guilford, 59
KERBY: Arthur, Sr., 18; James, 50
KEPNODLE: William, 24
KEY: Henry, 01
KIGHT: David, 15
KILLGORE: Rowland, 44
KINDRICK: Sylvanus, 16
KING: Berry, 06; Herom, 45; Isaac W., 25; John (R. Sol.), 54; Sarah, widow, 28
KINNAN: Austin, 59
KIRK: William, 11
KIRKLAND: John S., 26; Snowdon, 06
KIRKPATRICK: Harman, 05
KITLEY: Jesse, 44
KNOLES: Washington, 40
KNOWLES: Rice P., 12
KNOX?: James, (his orphans), 47
KOLB: Phillip, 04
LAMAR: Ezekiel, 21; John L., 14
LAMBERT: John, 04
LANCE: John R., minor, 08
LANDERS: Benjamin, 36
LANE: Elizabeth, widow, 60; Richard, 39
LANGLEY: Josiah, 47
LANGLY: James, 12
LANGSTON: William, 17
LANKFORD: James, 61
LAKRANCE: Joab, 02
LARY: William J., 57
LASSITER: John, 55
LAWHORN: Simeon (Sol. late war), 58
LAWSON: Dudley, 49
LAY: Sampson, 03
LEE: Archibald, 64; Joseph H., 55; Vincent L., 48; William, (his orphans), 60
LEONARD: William, 07
LESTER: Jacob, Jr., 36; John, 04
LEVERETT: Jesse, 8
LEVERETT: Joel P., 52
LEVINGSTON: Thomas, 21
LEWIS: Aaron, 55; Antonia, 52; William P., 10
LIGHTFOOT: James L., his orphs., 12; Thomas, 29
LILES: William, 47
LILEY: David, 65
LINDSEY: Thomas, his orphans, 43
LINSEYS: James, orphans, 28
LIVINGSTON: Thomas, 21
LOCKHART: Ellel, 31
LOCKS: John, orphans, 52
LON: Jesse, 38
LORD: Wheaten, 41
LOUGHRIDGE: Benjamin, 25
LOVE: Robert J., 43
LOWE: George T., 06
LOYD: Isham, 37
LUCAS: Charles, 31
LUCKETT: Thomas H., 31

LIVINGSTON: Martin, 41
LUKE: Abraham, 48
LUMPKIN: Robert D., 58; Samuel, 64
LUNDY: Thomas, (his orphans), 54
LUNSFORD: Elizabeth, widow, 21
LYNCH: Christopher, 49
LYONS: James H., 36
MACINTOSH: Rodrick, 09
MAHAFFEY: Hiram, 57
MAJORS: Eleanor, widow, 42
MALONE: Spencer, 30
MANGHAM: James W., 05
MANLEY: Jesse, 2
MANNER: Henry, 15
MAPP: Mary, (WRS) 53
MARCHMAN: John, 37; William R., 35
MARKSI: Jane L., widow, 47
MARSHALL: Mathew T., 18
MARTIN: Catherine, widow, 14; James E., 37; James V., 61; James, 19; John, 49; John, his orphans, 26; Levi, 51; William, 45
MASSEY: Simeon, 31
MATHALL: William T., 63
MATHEWS: Morris, 42
MATTHEWS: Phillip, 62
MATTOX: Nathan, 29
MAULDIN: Richard, 49
MAUEY: Henry, 49
MAXEY: Bennett H., 42; Jeremiah, 29
MAXWELL: Joel, 09
MAYFIELD: Obadiah, 20
MAYNOR: Recv H., 34
MAYO: Harmon, 36
MAYOR: Daniel, 61
MCARTHUR: Daniel, 41
MCBRIDE: James, Jr., 29
MCCALL: John, 11; Robert, 14
MCCANE: Thomas U., 23
MCCARTY: George W. B., orphans, 50
MCCLAIN: Ephraim, 26
MCCLENDON: Francis, 25; Moses 60; Stephen, 11
MCCLUNG: Reuben, 34; William W., 28
MCCOY: James, 33
MCCRIMMON: George, 51
MCCULLOCH: Hardy D., 33
MCDONALD: A. H., 16; Henry, 38; Norman, 06
MCDOWELL: Thomas C., 35; William, 58
MCDUGALL: Miles E., 04
MCEVER: Andrew, 32
MCFEE: Henderson, 32
MCGANGHEY: James, 05
MCGEE: Levin, 32; Patrick, 49; Wiley orp. of, 07
MCGEHEE: Abner, 07; Crawford, 18; John Wilson, 61
MCGIBBEN: Margaret (WRS), 54
MCGIBONEY: Erasmus, 13
MCINNIS: Joseph L., 52
MCGLANN: David, 53
MCGPAW: Joseph, 22
MCGUFFY: John, Jr., 28
MCKINNEY: Robert D., 05
MCKINNON: William, orphan, 42
MCKNIGHT: Samuel, 40
MCLAUGHIN: Gerrard, 25
MCLENDON: Joel, 27
MCLEOD: Archibald, 07; Hugh, orphan, 05
MCLEROY: Nathan, 22
MCMATH: Phillip, 21
MCMICHAEL: Griffin, 39; Silas, 55
MCMULLAN: Daniel, 43; Sinclair, 25
MCNEEL: William, 02
MCNEES: Samuel B., 12
MCQUEAN: John, 51
MCREE: Mary (W.R.S.), 57
MCOMB: Thornton, 60
MEDLIN: Riley, soldier, 47
MEDLOCK: John, 55
MELL: Benjamin (Orphans), 04; Thomas S., 63
MELTON: Eli, 52; Kinchen, 09
MENZIES: Archibald, 9
MEREDITH: Samuel, Jr., 01
MERRIT: Frederick, Jr., 43
METTS: Wright, 44
MICKLER: William, 39
MICES: Elijah, Sr., 21; Jared, 03; William, 18
MILLER: Bright, 50; Eli, 27; Frances, orp. 46; Henry, orp. 46; Jacob, 64; James, 03; Jedidiah S. (orphans), 58; Lucinda, orp., 46; Preston, 15; Solomon, orp. Thomas, orp. 46; William, 24, 57
MILLICAN: Charles W., 42; Hugh, 02
MILLS: Henry, 32; John B., 11
MINYARD: Fleming, 24
MITCHAM: John, 38
MITCHELL: Peter, 09; Roland, 26; Samuel J., 29; William, 17
MITCHUM: Hendrick, 31
NIXON: Jesse, 57

MOBLEY: Simpson P., 59
MONCRIEF: James, 30
MONK: Malone, 26
MONTGOMERY: John, 37
MOON: Ann Amella, widow, 19; Archelaus, 17; William, 47
MOORE: Daniel, 37; Elijah, Sr., 28; Thomas H., 53
MORAN: John B., 53
MORE: Alfred D., 35
MORGAN: David M., 47; James, 30; William, 43
MORRIS: Elizabeth, widow, 36; James, 49; Mary, wld., 18; William G., 27
MORTHALL: William T., 63
MOSE: David, 47
MOULTRIE: John B., 56; Joseph J., Revd., 22
MUNCREAP: David, 52
MURPHEY: Jeremiah, 42; William, 46
MURRAY: David Scott, 30; James W., 03
MURRILL: Martha, 43
MYERS: S., 43
MYNAND: Thomas, 43
NYLAN: Lewis, 09
NAILSWORTHY: William, 35
NARON: James H., 46
NARAMORE: Ellje W., 19
NASH: Edward L., 04; James Jr., 27
NEACE: George Sr., (R.S.), 60
NEALY: Stephen, 29
NEAL: William, 04
NEILL: Mac Rea, 15
NELSON: James F., 10
NEWBERRY: John, 62
NEWTON: Giles, 52
NICHOLS: William A., 34
NICHOLSON: Isaac, 02
NIGHT: Jessy, 37
NISBET: James, 23
NIX: John, 51; Joseph, 44
NOCKS: James (his orphans), 47
NOLEN: Elizabeth, widow, 55
NORMAN: Benjamin, 39
NORRIS: Archer, 16; Daniel N., 45
NORTH: Marcus D., 22
NORTON: James J., orphan, 12
NOWLIN: David, 56
NUNNERY: Henry, 36
NUTT: David M., 45
OBANION: Bryant, 58
O'CONNER: Patrick B., 18
O'DONNELL: Brian B., 58
OGLESBY: James A., 40
OGLETREE: David, 64; Philamon, 15
OLIN: Stephen, 35
OLIVER: Peter M., 56; Samuel, 19
OLLIFF: John, 26
ONEAL: Wootten, 25
OSBURN: David, 53
OTWELL: Gifford R., 30
OVERTON: James, 43; William B., 21
OWENBY: William (orphans), 60
OWENS: Andrew J., 51
PACE: Bassel, 29
PAGE: Jesse, his orphans, 23
PAINE: Winfred (Wid. R. S.), 58
PALMER: Martin, 37; Wilson, 46
PARHAM: Elijah, 28
PARI: Augustus M., 44
PARKER: L. Parker, 22; William H., 02
PARKERSON: John C., 53
PARR: Charles D., 55
PARRAMORE: Sarah, widow, 41
PARSONS: Robert, 32
PARTAIN: Robert, 0
PATE: Hollis M., 06; Stephen M., 40; Thomas, 58
PATERSON: P. V., 52
PATRIDGE: James, 58
PATTERSON: Alexander, 14; William, 03
PATTRICK: John, Sr., 53
PEARSON: Jeremiah, 27
PECK: Mary, widow, 34
PEEK: Robert, Jr., 15
PEEL: James, 40
PENDLEY: Hezekiah, 30
PENN: William S., 04
PEPPER: Kelley, 39
PERDEE: Larkin, 30
PERDUE: Newton, 24
PERKINS: John, 31
PERMINTER: William (soldier), 55
PERRY: Allen, 56; Peter, his orphs., 24; Terrill, (orphans), 58
PETER: Abnah, 19
PETERMAN: Henry G., 04
PETERS: John, 11
PETTIBONE: Mary, wld., 04
PHELPS: William W., 34
PHILLIPS: Ephraim, Sr., 45; John, 60
PIERCE: Sampson, 02; Thomas, 34

PINKSTON: Jesse M., 58
PIPER: James J., 07
PITMAN: Rene M., 03; Tilman R., 62
PITTMAN: Martin M., 28
PITTS: John D., 56
PLUMMER: Edward, 24
PONNELL: John, 07
PORTER: Elizabeth, (WRS), 54; John, 25
POSEY: Mire, orph., 29; William, 26
POTTER: Riel, 2
POTTS: William E., 26
POWELL: John, 21; Noah, 61; William, his orphans, 16; William, Jr., 41
PRATOR: John D., 14
PRATT: Daniel, 2
PRICE: William D., 44
PRICHARD: Pleasant, 08
PRICHETT: William M., 25
PRICKET: Josiah, 17; Thomas, 39
PUCKETT: John, 09
PURIFOY: Tillman, 54
PURNELL: Hope H., 61
RABUN: John, 52
RAGANA: Martha, widow, 12
RAGSDALE: Elijah, 26
RAHN: Johnathan, 26
RAINWATER: Abner, 06
RALSTON: David, 23
RAMSEY: Drury M., 62
RANDALL: John S., 33
RAWLS: William, 35
RAY: Dempsey J., 36; George, 62; Henry S., 61
REAVES: Irwin, 38
REED: Holland, 58; James, orphs., 10; William A., 34
REEDY: John B., 29; Mary, widow, 10
REESE: Benjamin, 63; Reuben, 06
REEVES: Abner, 34; James R., 23; Jesse, Orp., 63; John, 20; Thomas, 41
REGISTER: Sarah, widow, 34
REID: Nathaniel, 35; William, 58
RENFRO: Alfred, 35
RENFROE: John, 58
RENOLDS: John Jr., 48
REVEREL: Harpert B., 45
REYNOLDS: Benjamin (sol.), 62; Gabriel, 08; John, 59; Sharp, his orphs., 35; Thomas, his orphs., 48
RHODES: Hiram B., 1; James H., 62; William, 34
RICH: George W., 34
RICHARD: John, 35
RICHARDS: William M., 40
RICHARDSON: John, 31
RICHARSON: Thomas, 05
RICKERSON: Benjamin, Sr., 17
RIDDLE: Ann, orphan, 55; Elizabeth, orphan, 30; Tazv. or., 30
RIGANS: Mary, widow, 27
RIGGS: Stephen, 63
RIGGL: Wythe, 39
RILEY: Elizabeth, (widow), 01
ROBERTS: James, 10
ROBINSON: Alexander E., 62; Jesse, 35
ROCHE: John, 50
RODERICK: Joseph, 38
ROGUEMORE: Thomas J., 42
ROSS: Jesse M., 07
ROSSIE: John B., 19
ROST: Gasper, 5
ROWL: Jesse, 2
ROWLES: Jesse, 31
RUFF: William, 08
RUMSAY: Richard, 33
RUNNELLS: George W., 34
RUNNELS: Sarah T., widow, 25; Terry, 55
RUTHERFORD: Richard, orps. 04; William, 18
SAILERS: James, 15
SAILORS: William, 17
SAMPSON: Catherine J., 23
SANDEFORD: Elemlick, 52
SANDERLIN: Jesse, 20
SANDERS: Ambrose, 26; Augustus M., 14; David, 12; John, 35
SANFORD: Thomas P.,
SANFORD: Charles, 57; Jeremiah, 39; Jesse, 15
SANSENFIELD: John, Sr., 05; Larkin, 61
SAVAGE: Zachariah, 33
SAXON: David S., 32; John M., 09; Mary, 44
SCATES: William A., 04
SCARBOROUGH: Allen, 54; Perrin, 11
SCOTT: Asa, 59; John, 32; Josiah T., 14; William, 02
SEALE: Wm. H., 31
SEARS: David C., 10
SELF: John, N., 23
SHACKLEFORD: James L., 29; Joseph H., 27; Phillip, 29

SHANNON: Geo. M. W., orphan, 23; Mariah L., orphan, 23; Peter, orphan, 23
SHARP: Lewis J., 49
SHAW: William, 56
SHEFFIELD: William, Sr., 41
SHEFTALL: Emanuel, 32
SHELL: Green, 19
SHELMAN: Thomas P. C., 19
SHEPHERD: Mary Ann W., widow, 16; Nathan, 45; Thomas J., 10
SHERREN: John S., (orphans?), 62
SHERROD: James, 31
SHICK: John, Jr., 30
SHIELDS: James, 21
SHIPP: Abner, 30; Cannon H., 62; Wilshire L., 11
SIKES: William, 51
SIMMONS: William P., 20
SINCLAIRS: Robert F. (his orphans), 54
SINGLETON: Richard, 54
SINQUEFIELD: Mary, (widow),02
SIZEMORE: Henry, 09
SKINNER: Jesse M., orphan, 13; Jonathan, 16
SKIPPER: Bright, 50
SLATEN: Seaborn, 45
SLATER: James, 32
SLATEN: William, 39
SLATTER: Taliaferro B., 24; William C., 09
SLAUGHTER: James, 48
SLAYTON: John, 32
SMALLWOOD: Elijah, 23
SMAP: John L., 14
SMITH: Archibald, his orphans, 34; Edy, w:d., 08; Elijah, 31; Gideon H., Jr., 51; Griffin H., 21; Henry B., 11; Henry, Sr., 18; Howard, soldier, 47; Ira E., 47; Isaac, 36; James, 38; Jerrystone, 51; John G., 28; John, 36; Joseph, 61; Parker W., 42; Patin P., Rev., 48; Ransom, 26; Robert N., 37; Robert, 05, 39; Samuel, 16; Stephen, 11; William (orph.), 53; William P., 02
SNEAD: Robert R., 27
SNIDER: Anthony, 44
SNOW: George W., 19
SOLOMONS: Godwin, 38
SORRELL: John, 50
SORROW: Irven, (Sol.1784-1797), 62
SORROW: Elias W., 10
SOUTHERLAND: John, 06
SOUTHMAYD: Andrew, 25
SOWELL: Francis, 18
SPENCE: Alfred, 53; Joseph C., 34; Lewis, 06; Lucretia, widow, 27; McCalvis H., 01
SPENCER: James J., W., 05
SPOONER: Adam, 37
SPRING: James, 15
ST. JOHNS: Thomas, 33
STAFFORD: Anderson, 46
STALY: John, orphan, 13
STANFILL: Rahm, 26
STANFORD: Margaret, widow, 17
STANSELL: John W., 31
STARLING: William, 25
STARR: John, 58
STARRETT: Benjamin, 06
STATEN: James, 32
STATIGERY: John F., widower, 22
STEEL: Dennis, Jr., 05
STEPHENS: Allen, 18; Andrew B., orps., 04; James, 40; John, 41; Miles, 22; Oliver, 22
STEWART: Eli A., 28; J., 05; Thomas S., 51
STILLMAN: Samuel, 13
STINCHCOMB: Phillip, 05
STONE: Jenny, 63; John W., 32
STOVALL: Ozias, 09
STOWERS: Henry, 06
STRANGE: Benjamin, 24; William, 03
STRENGTH: James M., 44
STRICKLAND: John S., 18; Laddrick, 58
STRONG: Sherod, his orphans, 28
STROUD: Archibald J., W., 54
STROZIER: Peter, 37
STUART: Alexander, 37
STUBBLEFIELD: Catherine, widow, 49
STUBBS: A. F., orp., 51; James V., orp., 51
STUDDARD: Abraham, 64
SUMMERTIN: Thomas, Orph., 20
SUTHERLAND: James, 12
SWAN: William, 42
SWAR: John L., 14
SWEAPINGEN: Benjamin H., 19
SWILL: Sarah, widow, 45
TANNER: John, 40; Joseph, 03; William M., 22
TARROW: David, 16
TATE: John, 30; Samuel, 34; William, 04
TAYLOR: Jeremiah, Jr., 52; Nancy,

widow, 46; Susannah, widow, 20; Thomas, 45
TERRY: John W., 33; John, 31, 36
THIGPEN: James, 10; Malanton, 39
THOMAS: George W., 62; John S., 55; Patrick M., 63; Robert, 57; Septimus, 55; Stephens, Sr., 45; Willie W., 48
THOMASON: Anderson F., 61; Thomas G., 43; Thomas L., 39
THOMPSON: Daniel, 27; John D. (sol.), 57; John, 46; Nathan, 55; Richard, 02; William L., 31
THORNTON: Hastin G., 06; Vincent R., 29
THRASH: Voluntine, 22
THWEAT: Einchen P., 15; W. W., 03
TIDWELL: William, 44
TILLET: Leah, widow, 56
TIMMONS: Samuel, 06
TOLLS: William, 44
TOMLIN: Asariah, 17; Hezekiah W., 12
TONEY: Henricke, 32
TORNLIN: Hezekiah W., 12
TORRANCE: James, 19
TOWNSEND: James, 47; Thomas, Sr., 16
TRACY: Eleazer, his orphans, 40
TRANNAN: George W., 23
TRAP: Martha, widow, 10
TREADWELL: Isaac, 09
TREDAWAY: William, 13
TREWITT: Ira, 44
TROUP: James, 09
TROUT: Giles, 07
TUCKER: Anna, widow, 31; Elizabeth, widow, 37; Joel T., 38; Nathan, 54; William, 15
TUGGLE: John, Jr., 27
TURMAN: Joel C., 43, 44
TURNER: Andrew, his orphans, 40; Benjamin, 17; Green B.H., 10; Henry M., 51; James, 19; Micajah, 22; Shadrack, 42; Thomas, Sr., 16; William, 31; Zadock, 35
TWILLEY: James, 09
TYE: Daniel, 09
TYLER: Elizabeth (WRS), 51
VARDEMAN: William, 13
VAUGHN: Henry, 49; John, Jr., 57; Thos., 60
VEAL: Allen G., 06
VERDEL: Peter, 10
VINCENT: Jesse, 48
WADE: James, 17
WAGGONER: George B., 22
WAGON: George E., 59
WAITS: Jacob, 03
WAKEFIELD: Samuel, 26
WALDER: Samuel, 48
WALDROUP: Mathew, 39
WALDRUM: David M., 07
WALKER: Allen A., 15; David, 64; Ezekiel, 14; George W., 45; Jesse, Sr., 40; John, 48; Judith, widow, 41; Levin, 50; William, 60
WALLACE: David C., 08; William Sr., 09
WALKER: Benjamin, 38; Sarah, (W. R. S.), 62
WALLICE: Jesse, 55
WALLIS: Loveny, widow, 62; William C., 64
WAMMACK: Wiley, 14
WAMBLE: Allen B., 19
WAMMACK: William, 19
WARD: Thomas, 14; William, 38
WARREN: John, 43; William, 20
WARWICK: John, 51
WASHINGTON: Martha, widow, 26
WATERS: Henry, 19
WATKINS: James W., 30; John, 04; William, 36
WATSON: Elijah, 29; Elizabeth, (RS widow), 54; John M., soldier, 49; Joseph, 17; Tyre, 01
WATTS: John, 64; Rilant, 49
WAY: Wm. James, 62
WEIR: Daniel, 20
WELCH: Edward, 06; Michael, 04
WELBORN: John R., (orphans), 45
WELLS: Howell, 41
WHALEY: James, 33
WHEAT: Levi, 07
WHEELER: John W., 20; White, 13
WHIGHAM: John W., 17
WHITE: Cyrus, 20; Daniel, 19; David T., 39; James O., 41; James, 05; John, 17; Miller H., 21; Robert, 08; Thomas, 53
WHITEHEAD: Richard, 02; William, Sr., 33
WHITFIELD: William C., 23
WHITHURSTS: Lanfair (orphs), 56
WHITLOW: William, 37
WHORTON: Nicholas, 59
WHORTON: Isaac, 24
WICKER: Wiley W., 13
WIGGINS: John, 14; Willis, 22
WILDER: Eliza S., 'orph F.K.J.W.',

18; William, 62
WILHITE: John M., 62
WILKES: Solomon B., 31
WILKINS: David, 27; John, 21
WILKINSON: Selah, widow, 63
WILKISON: William A., 46
WILLIAMS: Arington B., 04; Charles G., 55; Henry H., 19; Hiram, 22; James R., 09; James, 22, 63; Jenkins D., 31; Jeremiah M., 60; Jesse, 36; John, 17; Lewis, 36; Robert B., 58; Solomon, 59; William, 24, 52; William, Jr., 48; Wilson, orphan, 42
WILLIAMSON: James, 07; Thomas E., 63; William, 28
WILLINGHAM: Isaac, Jr., 06
WILLIS: James, 28; Joshua, 41; Kissiah, widow, 64; Susannah (W.R.S.), 59
WILLSON: James, 35
WILSON: Andrew, orph., 31; Elizabeth (widow), 05; James, 28; Jeremiah, (sol), 53
WIMBERLY: Ezekiel, (soldier), 60
WINDHAM: William, 42
WINGATE: Amos, soldier, 50
WINNINGHAM: Abel, 57
WISDOM: Ellenor, widow, 27
WOLF: Council B., 46
WOLCOTT: Noah, 54
WOOD: John, 36; Mary (wid.), 61; Robert, 35; Sterling, 52; Thomas, his orphans, 10
WOODRUFF: William B., 44
WOOLEY: William, 57
WOOTEN: Simon, 49
WORTHALL: William T., 63
WRIGHT: David, 39; Elvira, wid., 36; Michael, 40; Samuel, (sol.), 59
WYATT: Thomas, 25
WYNN: John P., 63
YARBOROUGH: John H., 12; Lewis, 03
YATES: Joseph, 29
YORK: William, 22
YOUNG: Lucretia, widow, 36; Madison, 42; Michael, 19; Oran W. (orphans), 59
YOUNGBLOOD: Nathan, 36
ZUBER: Joshua, 57

www.ingramcontent.com/pod-product-compliance
Lightning Source LLC
Chambersburg PA
CBHW020059020526
44112CB00031B/491